Getting into

# Oxford & Cambridge

2013 entry

Jenny Blaiklock

# Getting Into guides

*Getting into Art & Design Courses*, 8th edition
*Getting into Business & Economics Courses*, 9th edition
*Getting into Dental School*, 7th edition
*Getting into Law*, 9th edition
*Getting into Medical School 2013 Entry*, 17th edition
*Getting into Physiotherapy Courses*, 6th edition
*Getting into Psychology Courses*, 9th edition
*Getting into US & Canadian Universities*, 2nd edition
*Getting into Veterinary School*, 8th edition
*How to Complete Your UCAS Application 2013 Entry*, 24th edition

*Getting into Oxford & Cambridge: 2013 entry*

This fifteenth edition published in 2012 by Trotman Publishing, an imprint of Crimson Publishing Ltd., Westminster House, Kew Road, Richmond, Surrey TW9 2ND

© Trotman Publishing 2008, 2009, 2010, 2011, 2012

© Trotman & Co Ltd 1987, 1989, 1991, 1994, 1996, 1999, 2001, 2003, 2005, 2007

**Author:** Jenny Blaiklock

Editions 13–14 by Katy Blatt
12th edition Sarah Alakija
11th edition Natalie Lancer
Editions 7–10 by Sarah Alakija

**British Library Cataloguing in Publication Data**
A catalogue record for this book is available from the British Library

ISBN 978 1 84455 476 8

Typeset by IDSUK (Data Connection) Ltd
Printed and bound in the UK by Ashford Colour Press, Gosport, Hants

# Contents

# Contents

# About the author

Jenny Blaiklock studied Philosophy, Politics and Economics at Oxford University, having worked as a researcher at the House of Lords for the Nuffield Trust. She spent 15 years in the advertising industry at McCann Erickson and Bartle Bogle Hegarty looking after clients as diverse as Levis, Smith & Nephew, Unilever, Liberty and Save the Children Fund.

She has since helped with fund-raising and event management for the NSPCC and Macmillan Cancer Support and is an adviser to a new charity, London Music Masters (LMM). The LMM Awards seek to help exceptionally talented young artists to further their professional careers while serving as positive role models, reaching new audiences and enriching their communities. The LMM Bridge Project is an educational initiative which identifies and nurtures young children who might not otherwise have the opportunity to engage in classical music.

In March 2010 she joined Mander Portman Woodward to oversee their Admissions, Marketing and Oxbridge Programme. Jenny has four children who have attended or are currently at Oxford and Cambridge, so has personal and practical experience of getting students into Oxbridge.

## Acknowledgements

Many thanks should go to all those who have previously written the Trotman guide to *Getting into Oxford & Cambridge*, particularly Sarah Charters and Katy Blatt. Thanks should also go to those who have given subject-specific advice, such as Steven Boyes, Simon Horner and Jim Burnett, and special thanks to those generous Oxbridge students who donated their personal statements and written case studies, especially Anthony Jack and Grace Blaiklock, Maddie Geddes-Barton, Nick Edwards and Harry Prebensen.

# Foreword

My own experience of getting into Oxford took place quite a few years ago. The reason I recount it here is to demonstrate that not everyone who is accepted into Oxbridge is a genius, or has parents who went there, or even does very well at their interview.

The phone in the hall rang. The lady from Admissions asked for me. She clearly enjoyed this aspect of her job. 'We're pleased to tell you that you've been offered a place to read PPE at St Hilda's,' she announced, pausing dramatically, anticipating my yelps of jubilation.

After uttering copious words of gratitude, I put down the receiver and raced into the kitchen where my mother was bent over the washing up. 'Guess what?' I spluttered, 'I've got into Oxford.' 'Have you, dear?' she said. 'That's wonderful.' Then she burst into tears because she didn't want me to leave home.

Later that evening my father returned from work. I gave him my news as soon as the front door opened. He seemed concerned and stated gravely, 'I don't think we should mention this in the family; you might make someone feel inadequate . . .'

My parents didn't really approve of further education for girls. It was all very well to be clever but their aspirations for me ran to getting a good job behind the counter of a local high street bank and with a bit of luck, the bank manager might take a shine to me and make me his wife.

My history teacher had other ideas. The inspirational Dame Celia Goodhart had just returned to teach part time at Queen's College and that year steered five of us into Oxbridge. My school was not particularly academic but specialised in producing interesting, spiky, opinionated girls with attitude.

Mrs Goodhart (as she was then) taught us how to question everything; how to read around your subject and do it because you were really interested in finding out more, not just because someone had told you that you needed to. One day I said to her in frustration, 'This topic is so difficult. The more I read and the more I think about the issues, the more I realise that there is too much to know and that I'll never be able to find the right answer.'

'Now we're getting somewhere,' she replied.

Getting into Oxbridge probably wasn't so difficult back then, especially for girls. The academic requirement was for five O levels (the equivalent of GCSEs) and two A levels. You had to sit the Oxbridge entrance test, which entailed writing some essays on your favoured subject. If you impressed the examiners, you were called for interview.

I knew nothing about the admissions process beyond what I had read in the literature available at my local library. I chose my college for probably all the wrong reasons. When I applied to Oxford, only five colleges were co-educational. I was determined, having spent my whole life in single-sex education, to branch out and embrace (hopefully literally) the opposite sex. I liked the rather medieval sound of one called Brasenose and it seemed to be located nice and centrally.

Medieval it certainly was. Despite my mother's admonitions to take some warm clothes, I arrived for my interview minimally equipped. I was shown to a room that looked like it had last been occupied by a 12th-century monk. Cotswold stone walls, a rickety bed with a very thin blanket, a viciously draughty mullion window and, as a concession to the 20th century, a tiny electric bar heater. I spent the night with my teeth chattering to themselves as I tried to not think about the interview scheduled for 9a.m. the next morning.

Tired and cold, I presented myself as requested. I was ushered into a large room to be faced by four tutors. In retrospect, I realised they were the philosophy, politics, economics and admission tutors. At the time they seemed like the Four Horsemen of the Apocalypse (without their horses, of course).

I still flush with embarrassment as I remind myself of the experience. In fact, I don't remember the details, just that at one point the economics tutor, sniffing out my level of mathematical ability, asked me, 'What is a logarithm?' I didn't have a clue. 'It's a number in a book,' I responded pathetically, knowing I was exposed to them all as a maths retard.

I returned to my cell and was joined by a friend. I was so stressed that I had a cigarette, even though I have never smoked before or since. Then I waited. I returned to check the noticeboard sporadically, as instructed. No news. A whole day went by. Still nothing. I found a phone box and told my parents that I didn't know when I'd be home. Another very cold night was spent in my cell. And then the next morning, after breakfast, I was told to report to St Hilda's.

Again, I don't remember much about my interview there but I do remember having a lovely chat with the economics tutor called Nita Watts who had been Keynes' right-hand woman at the Treasury. I was in awe. This woman had worked for John Maynard Keynes and if I was really lucky, she might be teaching me. We spent a long time talking about monetarism and why it might be intellectually and morally bankrupt. It was then I understood the privileged existence of the Oxbridge student. The cities are indeed beautiful, the buildings may be atmospheric and historic but it is the opportunity to be taught by some of the greatest minds in the world on a one-to-one basis that has to be the most mind-blowing privilege of all.

While I was studying at Oxford, several interesting work opportunities opened up for me. I was offered a job as a research assistant for the Nuffield Trust, examining Peers' voting habits at the House of Lords. I also took up a paid internship in the marketing department at Unilever. Both roles were enriching: both to my impoverished student pocket and to my CV later on.

A visit to the Oxford Appointments Office was seminal in my choice of career. Not having much of an idea of what I wanted to do after leaving university, I was advised by the helpful member of staff to use the careers library to find out about various professions that might interest me. I started at accounting. My maths had always been a weak point (see above) so I moved swiftly along the shelf to advertising. That sounded altogether much more fun and within three weeks I'd applied and been offered a job at McCann Erickson, who at the time were 'teaching the world to sing' with their Coca-Cola ads. Later, I moved to Bartle Bogle Hegarty, now a major force in the advertising sphere, when they were still in their infancy.

I loved my job but I loved having children even more and it took me over a decade to return to full-time employment. Over the past few years it has been a joy to watch my own children getting into Oxford and Cambridge. Really, the experience hasn't changed that much. It can be just as exhilarating, frustrating and nerve-wracking as I suspect it's always been. Working at Mander Portman Woodward, I feel privileged in being able to help our students through what can often seem a confusing and complex process and in reassuring them that if they've got what it takes, they will get in. If I did, so can you.

# Introduction

The title of this book says it all. Its purpose is to tell you everything you need to know to help you get into Oxford and Cambridge. It will also try to give you a flavour of what it's like to study there. My hope is that this book will help to demystify the whole application process and encourage you to apply if you feel you've got what it takes to get in.

You may already know quite a lot about the Oxbridge system and simply need a checklist of things you should do to ensure your best entry. This book certainly aims to be as comprehensive as possible and will cover all stages of the admissions procedure in detail.

You may know nothing at all about how to get in. Many potential applicants can be put off applying on the basis that Oxford or Cambridge somehow isn't right for them and that the odds of getting in are weighted towards students who have knowledge of a mythical 'old boys' network'. You would be wrong if you believe this. It is simply not true that Oxbridge operates in favour of those students who can somehow play the system. Having spoken to many admission tutors in researching this book, you can be guaranteed that your application will be judged on your potential to succeed and your willingness to work hard. The school you went to, how much money you have and how many of your ancestors went to Oxford or Cambridge count for nothing; getting in is about your academic potential alone.

You also shouldn't be dissuaded because you're worried that you're not a geeky Oxbridge type or that you're somehow not posh enough to hold your own there. Perhaps with all the publicity about the government wanting to encourage applications from state school pupils, you're worried that your application will be prejudiced because you go to an independent school. You shouldn't be concerned about this either. Both universities are keen to encourage applications from talented students whatever their background. If you're passionate about your subject and have the ability to excel at university, you're almost certainly a strong candidate for admission.

The aim of this book is to take you through the application process step by step: from making sure you're studying the right A levels in the first instance to giving you tips to help you sail through your interview.

**Chapter 1** explores why Oxford and Cambridge are so special and how they differ from other universities, giving the reader some idea of what it's like to study there. It also aims to demystify the selection process by outlining Oxbridge's equal opportunities policy. It explains the policy for disabled students; students with children; students from ethnic minorities; lesbian, gay and bisexual students; and educationally disadvantaged students or students who have had a disrupted education.

**Chapter 2** explains the financial aspects of studying at Oxbridge. Many students are put off by the idea that studying at Oxbridge is more expensive than at other universities. This chapter explains that this is not the case, and gives a breakdown of costs incurred over a year. The chapter also introduces the bursary schemes and music scholarships at the universities, and includes a case study of the spending habits of a new student at Cambridge.

**Chapter 3** discusses things you should consider well before the UCAS application. The chapter includes a section on choosing your A level subjects and the concept of 'facilitating' A levels. It also discusses the importance of high grades and the alternatives to UK A levels that are accepted by Oxford and Cambridge (including the Baccalaureate and Scottish Highers).

**Chapter 4** discusses the importance of choosing the right subject for you. Your choice of subject is more important than any other decision you will have to make during this process; more important than your choice of university and college. This chapter looks at the workload placed on students and the need to be prepared for this by reading widely and in depth. Also included in this section is a reading list that will give you a few ideas.

**Chapter 5** considers the best way to choose a university and college. It mentions the differences between Oxford and Cambridge, highlighting the importance of choosing the university that offers the subject that most suits you. Although this chapter refers to the Norrington and Tompkins Tables as points of reference (see Appendix 3), it advises against a tactical approach to college choice. Instead, it offers alternative methods for picking your future home. This chapter also explains the option of the 'open application'.

**Chapter 6** discusses the importance of extra-curricular experience in the application process. The option of a 'gap year' is considered, and how this 'time out' can be advantageous in some circumstances but disadvantageous in others. It looks at the importance of work experience, particularly if you wish to study a vocational subject at university, and how essential it is to be aware of events in your area, current affairs and news stories that are relevant to your chosen subject.

**Chapter 7** gives advice on UCAS and the personal statement. Suggestions are offered on how to make your application shine, as well as example statements with analysis. After you have completed your personal statement, Cambridge (but not Oxford) automatically sends a Supplementary Application Questionnaire (SAQ), and this chapter also gives advice on how to fill in this form. Many subjects require you to send in examples of written work and this section explains why written work is required, for which subjects essay submissions are usual and how best to satisfy the universities' requirements.

**Chapter 8** discusses the exams that are taken in addition to A levels for some subjects. These are taken either in advance of interviews or during the interview week in order to help interviewers decide on the best applicants. This chapter explains why these tests are necessary; gives lists of the subjects requiring additional testing at both Oxford and Cambridge; gives example questions, dates for testing and useful website links; and reading lists so that you can find out more for yourself.

**Chapter 9** explains the interview process. General information about interview practice is given, as well as a breakdown of what interviewers are looking for. In addition, there is information about different interview styles and how to deal with them; a comprehensive list of interview questions for a range of subjects; and six interview stories from previous applicants. Finally, there is a word of advice about presentation skills and an explanation of the pooling system.

**Chapter 10** discusses the application procedure for mature students and international students and gives information on specific issues relating to these categories.

**Chapter 11** looks at the final stages of the process: receiving an offer or coping with rejection; stress; and how you can make this experience a success, whether or not you obtain a place at Oxbridge.

In the appendices you will find: a useful timeline of the application process; a glossary of important terms; the Norrington and Tompkins Tables; and, finally, a map of both Oxford and Cambridge with the locations of the colleges marked.

# 1 | What studying at Oxford and Cambridge is really like

If you are considering an application to Oxford or Cambridge, you are probably keen to understand what makes these two universities such special places to study and why places are so fiercely fought over. This chapter will explain what sets Oxford and Cambridge apart from other universities and examines the advantages and disadvantages of studying there.

For over 800 years, Oxford and Cambridge have been the most distinguished centres of education in the world. The facilities and teaching are second to none and both have outstanding academic reputations. Not only that, both locations are beautiful, with a wealth of historic buildings and easy access to stunning countryside.

Oxford University is the oldest university in the English-speaking world and teaching has been taking place in Oxford since 1096. The University grew rapidly from 1167 when Henry II banned English students from attending the University of Paris. Former Oxford students include 26 British prime ministers, at least 30 international leaders, 26 Nobel Prize winners, seven current holders of the Order of Merit, at least six kings, 12 saints, 20 Archbishops of Canterbury and some 100 Olympic medal winners.

Early records suggest Cambridge University grew out of an association of scholars formed in 1209 in the city of Cambridge, after they left Oxford following a dispute with the townsfolk. Whilst it has not educated as many prime ministers as Oxford, it has produced 88 Nobel Prize winners. Over the course of its history, Cambridge University has built up a sizeable number of alumni who are notable in their fields, amongst them Samuel Pepys, John Maynard Keynes, Charles Darwin and Salman Rushdie. Perhaps most of all, the University is renowned for a long and distinguished tradition in mathematics and the sciences.

Importantly, both universities have some of the highest levels of graduate employment in the UK.

# Why study at Oxford or Cambridge?

## Oxford and Cambridge are always top of the university league tables

In 2011 the *Guardian* ran a survey that ranked UK universities according to teaching excellence (see Table 1, opposite page). Cambridge topped the league table with Oxford holding on to second place. The tables rank universities according to the following measures:

- how satisfied their final-year students are
- how much they spend per student
- the student/staff ratio
- the career prospects of their graduates
- a value-added score and what grades pupils have to achieve to stand a chance of being offered a place.

## The tutorial system

Unlike most universities, teaching at Oxford and Cambridge is built around the tutorial system. Tutorials (or supervisions as they are called at Cambridge) involve a meeting with your tutor, alone or with one or two other students, and generally last about an hour. Often, one of you will read your essay or written work aloud and this will act as a catalyst for discussion of the work that has been done independently during the week.

What makes an Oxbridge education so special is that you will have personal access to some of the world's experts in your chosen subject. Your tutor may be the person who actually 'wrote the book' on the subject you're studying, so being able to discuss topics with them in depth every week is an invaluable experience.

### Case study: Jack, New College, Oxford

Academically, the best thing about studying at Oxbridge is the tutorial system. At other universities your contact with your teachers may be minimal; at Oxford or Cambridge you will have at least one (more normally two) tutorials a week. These most often involve you and another student discussing your essays or problem sheets with your tutor. This is good because it means that you can't hide in the back of a lecture or seminar, thinking that you understand what's going on, only to realise when you get around to doing your exams that you really don't! At times the idea of having to justify yourself and your ideas can seem a bit stressful, but really you should see it as a fantastic opportunity to check with

**Table 1:** *Guardian* UK university league table 2011

| Rating | Previous year rating | Name of institution | Guardian score /100 | Satisfied overall (%) | Satisfied with teaching (%) | Satisfied with feedback (%) | Student: staff ratio | Spend per student (FTE) | Ave entry tariff | Value added score/10 | Career after 6 months |
|---|---|---|---|---|---|---|---|---|---|---|---|
| 1 | 2 | Cambridge | 100.0 | 91 | 90 | 72 | 11.7 | 9.76 | 556 | 6.0 | 82 |
| 2 | 1 | Oxford | 97.9 | 94 | 93 | 70 | 10.8 | 10 | 535 | 7.2 | 81 |
| 3 | 4 | St Andrews | 85.3 | 93 | 95 | 68 | 13.3 | 7.25 | 484 | 7.2 | 73 |
| 4 | 8 | London School of Economics | 84.7 | 80 | 81 | 63 | 11.8 | 8.45 | 512 | 6.0 | 81 |
| 5 | 5 | UCL | 82.5 | 87 | 87 | 62 | 9.7 | 8.43 | 474 | 7.5 | 77 |
| 6 | 3 | Warwick | 81.8 | 89 | 88 | 61 | 14.1 | 8.56 | 480 | 6.6 | 69 |
| 7 | 6 | Lancaster | 79.1 | 87 | 88 | 66 | 13.8 | 7.49 | 407 | 5.4 | 68 |
| 8 | 17 | Durham | 77.2 | 88 | 87 | 66 | 15.3 | 6.14 | 485 | 5.4 | 76 |
| 9 | 9 | Loughborough | 75.5 | 89 | 88 | 72 | 17.1 | 5.8 | 389 | 5.6 | 67 |
| 10 | 7 | Imperial College | 74.1 | 85 | 84 | 51 | 10.9 | 8.54 | 514 | 4.8 | 83 |

Source: *Guardian University Guide*

someone who really understands the subject that you haven't caught the wrong end of the stick.

The other great thing about studying at Oxford is the variety of interesting people you meet. Students come from a huge range of backgrounds and have about every conceivable extra-curricular interest, so you are bound to find plenty of people you get along with. What's more, almost everyone is really enthusiastic about their subject – without being overbearingly geeky – and that enthusiasm can be infectious.

## The colleges

Oxford and Cambridge colleges are an integral part of both universities. They are independent, self-governing communities of academics, students and staff.

The collegiate system is one of their strengths, giving students and academics the benefits of belonging to both a large, internationally renowned institution and to a smaller, interdisciplinary, academic college community. Colleges and halls enable leading academics and students across subjects and year groups, and from different cultures and countries, to come together and share ideas. Membership of an Oxbridge college, as well as a department or faculty, can add a whole new dimension to your university experience.

Your college can provide you with the perfect forum to discuss your work in seminars, over meals in the dining hall or in your room late into the evening. They'll help you to make friends quickly, and give you the opportunity to try a wide range of social and sporting activities.

All colleges invest heavily in facilities for library and IT provision, accommodation and pastoral care, and offer sports and social events. Undergraduate students benefit from the Junior Common Room (JCR) in their college – both a physical space and an organisation, it provides social events, advice and a link to the undergraduate community.

The relatively small number of students at each college means that you receive plenty of personal academic support. Each student has a college adviser, who is a member of the college's academic staff and who looks after the students throughout their time at college.

The standard of accommodation and food offered by some colleges is generally superior to that offered by most UK universities. Certain colleges have Michelin-starred chefs overseeing their kitchens, and wine cellars that equal some of the best clubs in the world. Unlike most universities, many colleges can accommodate you for the whole of your time at university, saving you the trouble and expense of finding your own accommodation.

## The best libraries and research facilities

Oxford and Cambridge are consistently placed among the highest ranked universities for their research performance and have been shown to outperform UK competitors in the scale and quality of their research across a wide range of subject areas.

The two universities also far outstrip other universities in terms of income from endowments and other private sources because of their age and their ability to attract funds from alumni and other donors.

Oxbridge students have access to the Bodleian (Oxford) and the Fitzwilliam (Cambridge) copyright libraries which hold a copy of every book, pamphlet, journal and magazine ever published in the UK. They are also non-lending, so students can always access the texts they need quickly, no matter how obscure. There are also hundreds of other libraries in Oxford and Cambridge, including at least one for each faculty and college.

## The people you'll meet

Contrary to popular belief, people who study at Oxford and Cambridge come from very diverse backgrounds and have many different interests and personalities. There really is no such thing as an 'Oxbridge type'. If you enjoy art, music, sport, acting, drinking, clubbing or just about any sort of activity imaginable, there will be many like-minded soulmates waiting to share your interests. Students come from private schools, state schools and from overseas. It's up to you to decide whether you want to spend your time punting along the river, attending May balls, writing for the university magazines, speaking at the Students' Union, drinking in the JCR or none of these things. Your Oxbridge experience is one only you can create; forget the clichés.

It is true, however, that Oxford and Cambridge attracts the highest performing undergraduate students, so you will be keeping company with some of the brightest people in the country and from abroad. They may not all become your friends or be your type but you are sure to find their company stimulating and intellectually satisfying.

## The location

Both Oxford and Cambridge are undeniably beautiful places to live and each has its own very special character.

Cambridge is much smaller than Oxford and has a market town feel about it. The university buildings are set much closer together, with a few exceptions such as Girton. Oxford feels more like a university set inside a city; colleges and faculty buildings are spaced out over a wider area and you will probably need a bike to get around easily.

Both universities have many beautiful buildings and each has its own architectural integrity. The colleges are stunning, whether you're into ancient architecture or modern chrome and glass.

### Case study: Emily, St John's College, Oxford

I never really thought very much about going to Oxford or Cambridge until after my GCSEs.

I was at a good comprehensive school and every year you'd hear about a few students who got into Oxford or Cambridge but most students went off happily to other universities and had a great time there.

I was surprised when I got a whole load of A*s for my GCSEs and then my teacher suggested that I think about applying to Oxbridge. She said that if I kept working hard and got good AS grades I'd have a good chance of getting in and should give it a go.

I didn't know anything about the application process and to be truthful neither did a lot of my teachers! I got all the information I needed off the internet. First I had to decide which uni was best for the subject I wanted to read. I thought human sciences sounded really interesting and as Oxford offered that, I decided to apply there.

Then there was all the stuff about which college to choose. I went to the faculty open day, which was really interesting as they talked us through exactly what the course entailed and what they were looking for in potential students. They also explained the admissions process, which was much less complicated than I imagined. We then had a chance to look around some colleges and following my visit I decided that St John's College suited me best because it was nice and central, large and well-endowed and had several fellows in my chosen subject.

I submitted my UCAS form in mid-October and luckily you don't have to take any written tests for human sciences. In early December I was called for interview and was offered a place just before Christmas.

What's it like now I'm here? It's wonderful. Hard work? Yes. Challenging? Yes. Stressful? Sometimes. But I wake up and look out of my window into the most beautiful quad and gaze at the buildings where people like me have been studying for hundreds of years. I am taught by the most fantastic tutors imaginable and I am fully involved in college life. I row, am a member of the University Biking Club and work part time in the JCR. I have made so many friendships that I'm sure will remain with me for the rest of my life.

If you are clever, if you love your subject and if you're willing to work hard, you should apply to Oxford.

## Employers are impressed by an Oxbridge degree

Whilst having a First Class degree will improve your employment prospects more than anything else, employers are always impressed by an Oxbridge degree. The tutorial system will have taught you many useful skills: how to formulate and articulate a logical point of view, how to work independently, how to assimilate large amounts of information and prepare for tight deadlines. Oxbridge graduates have the confidence, intellect and skills that employers are looking for.

It can also be easier to get an internship while you're studying at Oxbridge because the university terms are shorter and can be fitted around relevant work experience, and, if travel is your thing, you'll have long vacations in which to explore the world.

### Case study: Omar, Christ's College, Cambridge

During my second year at Cambridge, I applied for internships at the big accountancy firms and management consultants. It was a lot of work just doing the online tests and even more work preparing for the interviews. These companies take the interview process very seriously; someone told me that over 50% of their graduate trainees are students who have done internships with them while they were at university.

Most of the other candidates seemed to have experience of either economics or business studies; it was hard being the only historian in the group! However, by the time I'd had my third attempt, I had learnt that it was important to be properly prepared and I realised that it was not unlike getting ready for my weekly tutorial: I needed to do loads of reading to make sure I really understood the background of the company and the business that they were in and be ready to have a point of view on whatever questions they asked me.

That's why an Oxbridge education is so good. I have learnt to think on my feet and express my ideas orally. Also, I'm used to being surrounded by very clever people, so it's less intimidating than it might be for some students when you're confronted by MBAs and graduates from other universities.

And yes, I did get an internship on my fifth attempt!

### Are there any disadvantages?

The eight-week terms make your studying time very intensive and you will have to work hard outside of term too. Some students find the atmosphere highly pressured; you will constantly be called upon to meet deadlines and assimilate large amounts of information in a very short time. You will also have to balance your extra-curricular activities alongside your demanding academic schedule.

Neither of the universities allow undergraduate students to take part-time work (which should be taken into consideration when you're planning your finances), although there may be limited opportunities for paid employment within the college, for example in the libraries or JCR.

Some people will tell you that Oxford and Cambridge are not good places to go if you want to play masses of sport or be in a band or basically do anything other than study. It is certainly difficult to strike the right balance but many fine sportsmen and women, musicians, actors, artists and novelists have managed to do just that.

## Will it be suitable for me?

Just because Cambridge and Oxford are two of the leading universities in the world, this does not mean you should be daunted by their reputations. Their sole criterion for accepting new undergraduates is academic excellence. This is assessed through academic qualifications, during interviews and through special written tests prior to interview. If you have good academic qualifications and are passionate about learning, you are eligible and they will welcome your application.

### Students with disabilities and special educational needs (SEN)

Students with disabilities and SEN students are welcome at both universities and are in no way disadvantaged in their application. Disabilities must be declared on the UCAS form in order for the university and college to pool their resources and you must contact the admissions office at university and college level to discuss your individual needs.

For students with physical disabilities and impaired movement, living in older colleges can be tricky. Because Oxford and Cambridge are so old much of the architecture is 'listed', making it illegal to make changes to the buildings in any way. This means that it is sometimes impossible to install lifts. The same is true of some faculties, for example the architecture faculty at Cambridge. There are, however, many faculties with new buildings that do not pose such problems, and several colleges in both universities have recently been renovated. You will need to consult your chosen college to advise you on whether they are able to accommodate your needs.

Students with dyslexia are given the opportunity to write using a computer and extra time during exams; they should feel in no way anxious about applying. Those with visual or hearing impairments are also welcome to apply.

Each college should have a member of staff responsible for disabled students. You should ring the admissions tutor at your chosen college who will put you in touch with the disability staff member to discuss their resources and your needs. For more information see the links below.

- Cambridge Disability Resource Centre: www.admin.cam.ac.uk/univ/disability
- Oxford University Disability Advisory Service: www.admin.ox.ac.uk/eop/disab.

## Students with children

Both Oxford and Cambridge welcome applications from prospective students who have children. Several colleges provide accommodation for couples and families and some colleges have their own nurseries. There is also a university-wide nursery. You should ring the admissions office at your chosen college for more information.

The *Cambridge Guide for Student Parents* is written yearly by the Cambridge University Students' Union (CUSU) and is available online at www.cusu.cam.ac.uk/welfare/childcare.

Some colleges are also members of the Central Childcare Bursary Scheme that offers means-tested grants to overseas and EU students to help with the costs of childcare. Application forms are available from college offices, the Childcare Information Adviser and CUSU. There are two rounds of applications with closing dates on 1 November and 1 March each year.

Oxford University provides similar support, heavily subsidising the cost of local nursery care, as well as funding holiday play schemes. See www.admin.ox.ac.uk/childcare for further details.

## Students from ethnic minorities

It must be said that the number of students from ethnic minorities at Oxbridge is low. This has generated a large amount of bad press for both universities, perhaps undeservedly. Statistics show that the percentage of minority applicants accepted out of those who apply is very similar to the percentage of white Western applicants who are successful. This suggests that the cause of under-representation of ethnic minorities is primarily due to the lack of applications from these groups rather than a bias against them, and both universities have outreach policies that aim to attract students from under-represented groups.

Cambridge University states in its Equal Opportunity Policy and Codes of Practice that:

*'The University of Cambridge is committed in its pursuit of academic excellence to equality of opportunity and to a pro-active and inclusive approach to equality, which supports and encourages all under-represented groups, promotes an inclusive culture, and values diversity. [The University promises to] monitor the recruitment and progress of all students . . . paying particular attention to the recruitment and progress of ethnic minority students and staff.'*

*www.admin.cam.ac.uk/offices/hr/policy/equal.html*

In its Race Equality Policy, Oxford University states that:

*'The University of Oxford welcomes diversity amongst its students . . . recognising the contributions to the achievement of the University's mission that can be made by individuals from a wide range of backgrounds and experiences. The University aims to provide an inclusive environment which promotes equality, values diversity and maintains a working, learning and social environment in which the rights and dignity of all its . . . students are respected to assist them in reaching their full potential. The University will work to remove any barriers which might deter people of the highest potential and ability from applying to Oxford, either as staff or students.'*

*www.admin.ox.ac.uk/eop/policy/race/policy*

### Lesbian, gay, bisexual and transsexual (LGBT) students

Oxford and Cambridge are pluralist universities. Not only is there a central LGBT society at each university but each college also has its own LGBT representative. There are plenty of events to help you feel comfortable. For further information have a look at these websites:

- Cambridge: LesBiGay information from CUSU: www.lgbt.cusu. cam.ac.uk/
- Oxford: LesBiGay at OUSU: www.ousu.org/about/campaigns/a/lgbtq

### Educationally disadvantaged students or students who have had a disrupted education

Oxford and Cambridge are committed to helping applicants who have in some way been disadvantaged by a poor school education or by significant disruption to their educational career, which may have resulted in candidates getting lower grades at A level than they might otherwise have achieved.

Cambridge University, in particular, caters for these students with its Cambridge Special Access Scheme (CSAS). Admission tutors are keen to stress that applications are reviewed very thoroughly and each one is looked at on its merits; the Special Access Scheme allows teachers to complete a form that can explain extenuating circumstances in full.

On its website, Cambridge states that:

> 'The Cambridge Special Access Scheme (CSAS) is designed to ensure that applicants who have experienced particular personal, social or educational disadvantage can be accurately assessed.'

All colleges support the CSAS. You are eligible for the scheme if either of the following apply:

- few people from your school/college proceed to higher education AND your family has little or no tradition of studying for a degree;
- your education has been significantly disrupted or disadvantaged through health or personal problems, disability or difficulties with schooling.

To be considered under the scheme, you should apply in the normal way, but your referee should also complete the additional Special Access Scheme form by 15 October 2012. The form asks for additional information to enable applicants to be assessed more fairly and appropriate levels for conditional offers to be set.

> For more information about the CSAS, contact the Cambridge Admissions Office (telephone: 01223 764025; email: csas@cao. cam.ac.uk) or a college admissions office.

Oxford does not have an official Special Access Scheme but the University is keen to stress that special circumstances will be fully taken into consideration.

Oxford encourages teachers to include details of any special circumstances or other relevant information in the main UCAS application. Oxford also uses publicly available information to indicate those applicants who may have experienced educational or socio-economic disadvantages. Where applicants demonstrate the necessary academic aptitude for Oxford, they are strongly considered for interview, and seen in addition to students identified through the normal shortlisting process. For more information go to www.ox.ac.uk/undergraduate/finding_out_more/contextual_data.html.

# 2 | Money matters

This chapter will try to give you an idea of what it costs to study at Oxford and Cambridge. There is a commonly held misconception that an Oxbridge education is more expensive than other universities; however, this is not the case.

Both universities are keen to ensure that no talented student should be barred from studying with them because of the cost; and they are aware that the financial backgrounds of their applicants are varied. There are generous bursary schemes available if you are facing financial difficulty – most colleges want to take the best students regardless of income and don't want money worries distracting you from your degree.

Accommodation in both cities is expensive compared to other regional universities but many colleges provide accommodation for their students for all three or four years of their courses. Oxford suggests budgeting £6,600 per year for private rentals, which includes around £1,000 in utility bills.

If cost is a consideration, you should ensure that the college you choose offers accommodation for the whole of your course as 'living in' is generally cheaper than 'living out'.

Living expenses are generally in line with other universities in the south of England.

## The cost of studying at Oxbridge

### Tuition fees

The University of Cambridge will charge a tuition fee of £9,000 per year for all new UK and EU students starting courses in 2012. Many students will be eligible for support, meaning that their tuition fee could be as low as £6,000 per year.

The University of Oxford's proposed tuition charge per year of undergraduate study starting from 2012 is between £3,500 and £9,000 depending on household income. English students from a household income of less than £25,000 will receive a reduction in their tuition charge. English students from a household income of less than £42,600 will receive a bursary.

## Living expenses

As a guideline, Oxford gives the following: accommodation in college around £3,700 per year, food £1,750, other living costs £1,850 (entertainment £780, clothes £430, course costs £290, travel from home £220, miscellaneous £130).

Cambridge indicate that students should budget £7,170 a year: accommodation £70–£120 per week, kitchen facilities £12–£17 per week, meals £3–£4 per day.

At both universities, you may prefer to make your own food rather than eat in Hall all the time. Most colleges have adequate kitchen facilities and you can buy fresh food from the local markets and supermarkets quite cheaply.

You will also need to budget a small amount each week to do your laundry. Most colleges have a laundry room with washing machines and tumble dryers and these cost approximately £3.

## Transport

You won't need to spend money getting around the university as both are easily navigable by bike or on foot.

If it is raining some students prefer to take the bus to their lectures at a cost of about £1 per ride. However, most students cycle everywhere. This is by far the fastest and the cheapest way to travel. If you don't have a bike already you can pick one up from one of the many second-hand bike shops in both cities from as little as £35 (although if you want a better ride you will obviously have to pay more). Additional costs to consider when investing in a bike include: the helmet at approximately £25; locking systems to prevent theft (very important) at about £15–£20; and servicing charges. There are many bike mechanics across both cities who will fix your bike for a fee. However, college porters usually have free bike repair kits and there are normally bike reps at each college: students who you can call on for help mending and servicing your wheels for absolutely no charge.

## Study materials

Most books that you'll need are available at college and university libraries, so your expenses should be limited to the usual items of stationery that you had at school. Unless you're specifically instructed to buy books by your faculty, it's probably best to wait until you arrive before spending lots of money unnecessarily.

You will probably want to purchase a laptop, if you don't already own one.

Scientists may need to purchase lab coats and mathematicians may need to buy calculators. Again, you will be told by the college if you need any specific study materials for your course.

---

**Case study: Grace, Trinity College, Cambridge**

One of the things that changes when you go to university is that you have to organise your own finances and learning how to budget can be a challenge at first! Making a note of how much you're spending on food, books, clothes and going out per week can be an effective way of keeping track of your finances.

For my accommodation I pay a termly bill direct to my college. Prices vary according to each college and the size and location of your room. I am lucky enough to have a room in college for all three years of my course, but other smaller colleges offer their students outside accommodation as they don't have enough space in college. Prices range from about £800–£1,500 per term; you pay more for a larger room or one with en-suite facilities.

Some people choose to cook for themselves in the facilities provided, but these can be fairly minimal so an easier option is often Hall. All colleges have Formal Hall and then a cheaper canteen option. Prices again vary depending on what college you're at, but a Formal Hall ticket is around £8 for a three-course meal with wine, and a meal at the Buttery can range from £3–£5 depending on how much you get. There is also the college bar where you can get snacks and coffees at much cheaper prices than at Café Nero or Starbucks. A good and bad aspect of eating in college is that you pay for it using your university card. While this is convenient and means you don't have to pay with cash, it is harder to keep track of just how much you're spending on food. However, most students will go to Hall or Buttery as it is a nice break from work to sit down for lunch or dinner with friends.

I would say I spend around £120 a week while I'm in Cambridge. This obviously varies week to week and will be considerably more if I'm going out a lot. The most important thing is to keep an eye on how much you're spending as you go through term so you don't get a big shock at the end when your college bill is sent to you.

---

> ### Case study: One parent's view on the cost of studying at Oxford
>
> My son John was financed through Oxford by a combination of student loan and subsidy from me. In his first year the former paid for his tuition fees and accommodation with a little left over for pocket money. As I pay for his mobile contract and clothes, I then provided about £100 per week to cover his food and drink, entertainment and books during term time and encouraged him to keep a diary of how much he was spending so that, by trial and error, each term I would be better able to gauge how much would be sufficient. Unfortunately, this never happened. John was a voracious acquirer of books and I seemed to be continually transferring money into his bank account to support his habit.
>
> In his second and subsequent years he lived out, which is more expensive than living in college. As a result, the maintenance loan was insufficient to cover his accommodation costs, which were increased by deposits that were inevitably not returned in full and the costs of gas and electricity, as well as internet connections. The latter was the most expensive known to man. In addition, it required a connection at the start of the tenancy and disconnection at the end, for an additional charge of course.
>
> With the benefit of the experience of financing John's four years at Oxford, I would try to persuade his siblings to stay in residence as this is significantly cheaper. In addition, I would start with what might be a relatively low weekly allowance and adjust it as I know they will shout if the money runs out, whereas you never know if you pay them too much!
>
> (John attended New College, Oxford)

## Financial support and bursaries

Cambridge states that it is:

> 'committed to the principle that no suitably qualified UK student should be deterred by their financial circumstances from applying to Cambridge, and that no student should have to leave because of financial difficulties.
>
> The University therefore plans to provide one of the most extensive and flexible support packages in the country to ensure that a Cambridge education is accessible to all, regardless of background.

*This will include the provision of Cambridge Bursaries of £3,500 per year to all UK students from families with incomes below £25,000 per year. UK students from families with household incomes between £25,000 and £42,000 per year will receive a lower level of Cambridge Bursary each year.*

*Cambridge Bursaries do not need to be repaid and students can choose to take them either as a bursary to help with their living costs or to reduce their tuition fees by £3,000 each year.*

*A higher Bursary of £5,650 per year will be available to UK mature students with family incomes below £25,000 per year who are also resident in Cambridge throughout the year.*

*The University also intends to provide students from particularly disadvantaged backgrounds with additional fee waivers of £6,000 in their first year through the National Scholarship Programme.'*

Oxford says that it:

*'remains committed to ensuring that UK students with the academic ability to obtain a place at Oxford are able to do so regardless of their background. While many universities are offering either fee waivers or bursaries in response to the new tuition charges, Oxford will provide both. Oxford is offering the most generous financial support of any university to those on a family income of less than £16,000.*

*This University is proud to be able to offer a generous financial support package for students from the lowest-income households starting their undergraduate studies here in 2012. Remember, this will be in addition to the support available from the government.*

What will this mean?

- The top support from Oxford will total £10,000 in the first year and over £6,000 in every later year.
- Based on current student profiles, one in six students will receive a fee waiver and a quarter will receive a bursary.'

For more information on the financial support available, check out the following websites.

Cambridge:

- www.cam.ac.uk/admissions/undergraduate/finance
- www.admin.cam.ac.uk/univ/cambridgebursary

Oxford:

- www.ox.ac.uk/admissions/undergraduate_courses/student_funding

## Music awards and scholarships

Both universities are well known for the excellence and diversity of their music-making. One of the ways they maintain their high standards of musicianship is by offering music awards to students. Music award holders are amongst the hardest working students in the universities, as they have to juggle extensive musical commitments with their academic studies. The experience they gain is huge, though, and the opportunity to sing with, play in orchestras with or conduct some of the best young musicians in the country is unique. Many award holders go on to careers in music.

If you're a talented musician, it is worth considering applying for a scholarship. The way you apply is different from the normal route and needs careful explanation. At both universities you can apply for organ or choral scholarships and there are some special awards for repetiteurs and chamber music.

Most colleges have open days where you can find out more about the awards and you are strongly advised to attend them to better understand the application process. You will also have the opportunity of meeting current music award holders and visiting the colleges to see their facilities for music making.

Auditions generally take place in September and an offer of a choral or organ scholarship does not guarantee you a place at a college as you will still need to go through the normal admission procedure and achieve the necessary grades.

For more information visit:

Cambridge:

- www.cam.ac.uk/admissions/undergraduate/musicawards

Oxford:

- www.music.ox.ac.uk/admissions/organ-and-choral-scholarships1.

### Choral awards

In all, 16 colleges at Oxford and 21 colleges at Cambridge offer choral awards, covering the whole range of voices: sopranos, contraltos, countertenors, tenors, baritones and basses. The basic duty of choral scholars is to sing at chapel services, but their involvement in college and university music goes further than this, extending to solo work, chamber groups and choruses. These and several of the mixed-voice choirs undertake concerts, tours and recordings, with some of these activities falling within the vacation periods. A number of colleges offer singing lessons as part of the award.

### Case study: Nick, St John's, Cambridge

I decided to apply to be a choral scholar in the final year of my GCSEs, primarily because I had immensely enjoyed singing in the school choir for the previous four years. I wasn't a chorister as a child, and I think it's important to emphasise that you don't necessarily need to come from the traditional 'chorister at St Paul's/Westminster' background. However, my school did have a very good track record when it came to getting singers into Oxbridge choral scholarships. The most valuable preparation for me was twice being sent to sing informally for the Director of Music at St John's; the feedback was invaluable and it meant that I was more comfortable singing for him in the actual choral trials. In addition to this, my school gave me lots of interview preparation which proved to be very useful.

Perhaps the highlight of the Cambridge choral scholar experience is, for me at least, going on tour in the holidays. Most colleges will have at least one international tour a year, and at some colleges you get paid pretty well! The only downside to the tour experience is that it really eats into your revision time in the Easter holidays. If you're planning to do a very high-workload subject (medicine, for example) then I would seriously consider applying to a college that perhaps is less of a commitment than St John's.

Being a choral scholar at St John's certainly takes up a lot of time and if you're looking for less of a commitment, apply to colleges that don't have seven services a week. There are plenty of fantastic choirs in Cambridge and Oxford that don't sing as much as St John's and Kings. I earn a minimum of around £1,600 a year from the choir, although the figure is usually larger than that as we get paid to go on tour. In addition, I sing in the Gents of St John's (a close harmony group made up from the back row of the choir) which is actually far more lucrative than the choir itself!

To summarise, if you think you're a good enough singer to be awarded a choral scholarship, then you probably are! Almost all the Directors of Music will be happy to arrange an informal meeting where you can sing to them, and they can give you useful advice (possibly the most valuable advice you'll get). Whether you choose a college with a well-known, high-commitment choir or a smaller college with fewer services, you'll always find fantastic singing opportunities at Oxbridge as a choral scholar. I have never met a choral scholar who regretted their decision to sing at university, whatever the college.

### Organ awards

Organ scholarships are offered by many colleges. The organ scholar is responsible for running the chapel music where there is no music tutor involved, and also for playing a leading part in the college's musical life in general. The experience is invaluable for musicians interested in directing and organising musical activities across a wide spectrum. Colleges normally assist in the cost of organ lessons.

### Repetiteur scholarships

The repetiteur scholarship is open to pianists who are interested in coaching singers. It is offered jointly by St Catherine's College, Oxford and New Chamber Opera. This offers the possibility of extensive experience as a repetiteur in the musical theatre.

Some colleges will not allow students studying certain subjects to be music scholars because the academic demands of their courses are too great.

Anyone wishing to apply for a music award needs to read the relevant university and college websites very carefully for full details of the awards and the application process.

- www.cam.ac.uk/admissions/undergraduate/musicawards/.
- www.music.ox.ac.uk/admissions/organ-and-choral-scholarships1/Organandchoralscholarships-main-page.html.

# 3 | Entry requirements

By now you may have decided that you'd like to apply to Oxford or Cambridge. How do you know if you're a suitable candidate and if you have a realistic chance of getting in?

It goes without saying that entry is very competitive and we've all read stories in the newspapers about students with perfect grades failing to get a place and others with lesser grades somehow being successful. It's important to understand the facts and forget the fiction.

Oxford University makes conditional offers for students studying A levels ranging between A*A*A and AAA (or 38–40 points in the International Baccalaureate including core points, or AAAAB/AAAAA in Scottish Highers, or another equivalent) depending on the subject. Specific A level (or equivalent) subjects may be required to apply for some subjects, especially in the sciences, and some subjects require applicants to sit a written test or submit written work.

Cambridge colleges will require A*AA in three A level subjects (or equivalent), although they have the discretion to make non-standard offers where appropriate as part of their holistic assessment of candidates. Applicants may be asked to submit written work or sit a test (i.e. BMAT or a college-based test).

Both universities interview the majority of undergraduate applicants.

So here are some important questions to consider before you apply.

## Are you studying the right subjects?

The AS and A level subject choices you make in Year 11 (or equivalent) can have a significant impact on the course options available to you at university.

In 2011, the Russell Group, who represents the leading 20 UK universities (including Oxford and Cambridge), published its first ever detailed guide to post-16 subject choices, *Informed Choices*. This report should now be obligatory reading for every A level candidate (www.russellgroup.ac.uk/informed-choices.aspx).

*Informed Choices*, produced in collaboration with the Institute of Career Guidance, is aimed at all students considering A level and equivalent options. It includes advice on the best subject combinations for a wide range of university courses as well as advice on the best choices if you don't know what you want to study after school and need to keep your options open.

*Informed Choices* lists the so-called 'facilitating' subjects. These are the ones that they judge to be the most effective for gaining a place at university. They are:

- mathematics
- English
- geography
- history
- biology
- chemistry
- physics
- classical or modern foreign languages.

The guide states that even where these choices are not specified as required subjects, universities may still have a preference for them.

It warns: 'If you decide not to choose some of the facilitating subjects at advanced level, many degrees at competitive universities will not be open to you.'

The guide says students who decide to take more than one 'soft' subject should be cautious. It suggests the 'soft' subjects are those with a vocational or practical bent, and lists examples as media studies, art and design, photography and business studies.

When the Oxford and Cambridge admissions tutors assess candidates, they consider not only the individual A level (or equivalent) subjects taken but also the combination of subjects. Generally they prefer applicants to have taken certain subjects or combinations of subjects which they feel will help their studies once they arrive at their universities. Recommended subjects required by Oxford and Cambridge are in accordance with the *Informed Choices* list.

Many Oxford and Cambridge courses require prior knowledge of certain subjects, and Oxford will expect such subjects to be passed normally with at least an A grade at A level or equivalent and Cambridge with either one or two A*s and an A.

If you have already decided on a course that you would like to study at university, it's recommended that you review the information given on the Oxford and Cambridge websites (www.cam.ac.uk/admissions/undergraduaterequirements and www.ox.ac.uk/admissions/undergraduaterequirements) before you finalise your A level subject choices, to check that they will be appropriate for an Oxbridge application.

Some students chose to take two arts and two science subjects at AS level because they believe it will keep their options open. While such a subject combination does provide a suitable preparation for many arts and social science courses at university, you should be aware that it can make you a less competitive applicant for broad-based science courses.

Some A level subjects are considered either essential or useful for a number of courses at Oxbridge, therefore choosing one or more of these will help keep your options open. These subjects include: chemistry, English literature, history, languages, mathematics, physics, further mathematics and biology.

## Arts and social science courses

If you are undecided about which arts or social sciences course you'd like to study at university, then English literature, history, languages and mathematics are good 'facilitating' subjects: choosing one or more of these will provide a good foundation for your subject combination.

Other good choices to combine with these subjects include: an additional language, ancient history, classical civilisation, economics, further mathematics, geography, philosophy, religious studies and sciences (biology, chemistry or physics).

Other possible subject choices might be archaeology, citizenship, English language, environmental science, government and politics, history of art, law, music, psychology or sociology.

## Science courses

If you are interested in studying a science course at university but you are not sure which one, you are advised to take at least two, and ideally three, of biology, chemistry, mathematics and physics. Some pairings of these subjects are more natural than others. The most natural pairs are biology and chemistry, chemistry and physics, and mathematics and physics.

In practice, the vast majority of applicants for science courses at Oxbridge take at least three of these subjects. Another useful combination is mathematics, further mathematics and physics. Many students take four of biology, chemistry, mathematics, further mathematics and physics.

If you are planning to study biological or medical sciences you should take chemistry; for physical sciences or engineering you should take mathematics and physics and ideally further mathematics.

Other possible subject choices, for instance computing, design and technology, electronics or psychology, may be useful preparation for some science courses.

> ### Other A level subjects
>
> There are other subjects not mentioned above such as general studies and critical thinking, but Oxford and Cambridge will usually only consider these as a fourth A level subject.

## Do you have the right qualifications?

There are no set 'grade requirements' for applying to Oxbridge but that doesn't mean that you don't have to be an excellent student to gain a place. Oxford and Cambridge are considered Britain's 'elite' universities; in the words of one Cambridge admissions tutor: 'We are the best university in the world and we want the best undergraduates in the world.'

You will need consistently high grades, a glowing reference from your current school or college, and be able to demonstrate commitment to your chosen course in your personal statement and interview. Each year, thousands of students apply for a place at both universities (over 30,000 in 2010); competition is understandably intense and the success ratio is approximately 5:1. However, this should not put you off trying if you fulfil the universities' basic requirements. Remember, someone has to get in and not everyone who applies is a genius. To state the obvious: if you don't apply, you won't get in!

Set out below is information given by the Oxford and Cambridge websites regarding their requirements for an offer of a place.

### Cambridge requirements in detail

Although the website mainly talks in terms of GCSEs and A levels, other school and national examinations at an equivalent level are equally acceptable. Whatever system you're being educated in, Cambridge requires top grades in the highest level qualifications available for school students. Most of the information below has been taken from the Cambridge admissions website (www.cam.ac.uk/admissions/undergraduate/).

If you are taking any other examination system (including the Advanced International Certificate of Education offered by Cambridge Assessment), it is a good idea to make early contact with the Cambridge Admissions Office to check that it provides an appropriate preparation for the course you hope to study.

**AS levels:** Cambridge applicants are encouraged to study either four or five AS levels in Year 12 and they normally expect high A grades in relevant subjects at AS level. Applicants taking five subjects won't be at an advantage compared with those taking four. Separate certification at AS level in the case of subjects being studied at A level isn't required and applicants not cashing in AS levels won't be disadvantaged. All applicants are asked to report (in the Supplementary Application Questionnaire) the results of all AS and A level modules taken to date, whether certificated or not. Colleges won't make unconditional offers on the basis of AS level grades alone.

**A levels:** Most applicants to Cambridge are studying three or four A level subjects. As has been the case for the last two years, the standard conditional A level offer for 2013 entry will be A*AA. The subject in which the A* is to be achieved is unlikely to be specified in most cases.

All colleges modify offers to take account of individual circumstances. For example, lower offers may be made to students applying through the Cambridge Special Access Scheme whose potential hasn't been realised at school because of significant educational or personal disadvantage. On the other hand, more challenging offers may be set where some doubt exists and the alternative is no offer.

**Extended project:** The extended project is a separate qualification that A level students may add to their study programme. Students carry out a project on a topic of their choosing, which may or may not be linked to their chosen A level subjects. The projects involve planning, research and evaluation, but the end product may be in the form of a dissertation, a performance or an artefact. The aim of the extended project is to develop research and independent learning skills that will be of great benefit in higher education and employment. Currently neither university uses the extended project in its offers, but they recognise the benefits: the skills which can ease the transition from secondary to higher education.

Cambridge has stated that the extended project may be a suitable topic for discussion at interview and in some cases, where it is relevant, it may be an appropriate piece of written work to be submitted.

**AQA Baccalaureate:** Applicants taking the AQA Baccalaureate should note that this is an acceptable qualification for entry to Cambridge. However, offers will be conditional on achievement in the A levels within the qualification rather than the overall Baccalaureate award.

**Cambridge Pre-U:** Cambridge Pre-U is a post-16 qualification designed to prepare students with the important skills needed at university. It challenges students to show not only a keen grasp of their subject, but also lateral, critical and contextual thinking. It encourages independent research and promotes learning through innovative approaches to the curriculum and assessment. Both universities will accept the Pre-U but express no preference for it over any other qualification.

Students who are either studying towards the full Cambridge Pre-U Diploma or certain Principal Subjects within the qualification alongside A levels are eligible to apply. Conditional offers are set on an individual basis but are likely to include achieving Distinction level grades (D2 or D3) in Principal Subjects.

**International Baccalaureate Diploma Programme:** Offers are regularly made on the International Baccalaureate, requiring scores between 40 and 42 points out of 45, with 776 or 777 in the Higher Level subjects. For advice about suitable subject choices, see the course requirements on the Cambridge website. Please note that for these purposes, Standard Level subjects are broadly comparable to AS levels and Higher Level subjects to A levels.

**Scottish Highers and Advanced Highers:** Cambridge normally expect applicants with Scottish qualifications to have achieved a minimum of four A grades at Higher Grade, plus Advanced Highers. Offers will usually require AAA in three Advanced Highers. In some cases two Advanced Highers and an additional Higher may be acceptable. For advice about suitable subject choices, see the course requirements on the Cambridge website. Please note that for these purposes, Highers are broadly comparable to AS level subjects and Advanced Highers to A levels.

If you're studying towards a Scottish Baccalaureate qualification you're expected to offer three Advanced Highers as part of it.

Applicants who are prevented from studying more than two Advanced Highers due to reasons outside their control are considered on a case-by-case basis and are advised to contact the college to which they intend to apply as early as possible.

**Welsh Baccalaureate:** Applicants taking the Advanced Diploma in the Welsh Baccalaureate are expected to have studied three subjects at A level as part of their qualification. Offers are conditional on achievement in the A levels within the qualification rather than the overall Baccalaureate award (see AS/A levels guidance above).

**Irish Leaving Certificate:** Applicants from the Republic of Ireland who are studying towards the Irish Leaving Certificate are eligible to apply. A typical offer for the Irish Leaving Certificate is AAAAA at Higher Level.

Applicants for Medicine and Veterinary Medicine may be asked to take an IGCSE (International General Certificate of Secondary Education) or equivalent in the science subject not taken within the Irish Leaving Certificate.

**Access to HE Diploma:** Applicants to Cambridge studying the Access to HE Diploma are generally expected to achieve a standard equivalent to conditional A level offers. Therefore, a typical offer would require attainment of the Access to HE Diploma with Distinctions in all relevant subject units. Applicants may be asked to meet certain subject-specific requirements as well, such as an additional A level in Mathematics or demonstration of an aptitude for languages.

**European Baccalaureate:** If you are studying towards the European Baccalaureate, please note that successful applicants are typically asked for 85–90% overall, with 90% in those subjects relating most closely to the course they wish to study.

**French Baccalaureate:** Typical offers for applicants taking the French Baccalaureate (including the International Option) are 16 or 17 ('mention très bien') out of 20. Applicants are also usually asked to achieve 16 or 17 in specific subjects.

**German Abitur:** If you are studying towards the German Abitur, please note that applicants are typically asked for an overall score of between 1.0 and 1.3, with 14 or 15 in those subjects that relate most closely to the course they wish to study.

**SATs and Advanced Placement Tests:** Prospective applicants from Canada and the USA taking SATs and Advanced Placement Tests should note that offers are usually made on an individual basis. In addition to high passes in the High School Diploma and the SAT, successful applicants should have normally achieved Grade 5 in at least five Advanced Placement Tests in appropriate subjects.

**Diplomas:** Only the Advanced Diplomas in Engineering, Manufacturing and Product Design, and Environmental and Land-based Studies provide appropriate preparation for certain Cambridge courses, and are acceptable for entry as detailed below.

- The Advanced Diplomas in Engineering and in Manufacturing and Product Design are acceptable for Engineering as long as you have taken specified options within the Additional Specialist Learning component.
- The Advanced Diploma in Environmental and Land-based Studies is acceptable for Geography, Land Economy and Natural Sciences (Biological) as long as you have taken two appropriate A levels within the Additional Specialist Learning component. In the case of Natural Sciences (Biological), these should be A level Chemistry and either Biology, Mathematics or Physics A level. The requirements for Geography and Land Economy are more flexible.

**VCE and Applied A Levels, GNVQs and BTECs:** VCE A levels, Applied A levels, GNVQs and/or BTECs are not an ideal preparation for most Cambridge courses, where the emphasis is more academic than vocational. As such, these qualifications cannot, unless otherwise stated, be used to replace the 'essential' and 'highly desirable' A level subjects listed for each course. However, if the 'essential' and 'highly desirable' subjects are covered, a six-unit VCE or Applied A level could be taken instead of a third A level or as an additional fourth broadening subject.

This combination of A levels and VCE or other qualifications may be acceptable for some courses. Potential applicants taking these qualifications are advised to seek further advice from a college admissions tutor.

## Oxford requirements in detail

Most of the information below has been taken from the Oxford admissions website. Many students who apply to Oxford are taking A levels but any candidate who has already taken, or who is currently studying any other equivalent qualifications is also most welcome to apply.

The information below outlines the general entrance requirements.

**A levels:** Oxford make conditional offers to applicants of between A\*A\*A and AAA depending on the subject.

Admission tutors stress that as long as you meet the requirements set out by the colleges, any subject except for general studies is an approved option. They do not require students to disclose their unit grades on their UCAS application and any offer they make will be based on the final grades you achieve at A2 level.

**Extended projects:** Although the University recognises that the extended project (EP) gives a student the opportunity to work on their chosen subject in greater depth, thus developing their research and academic skills, it will not be regarded as a condition of any offer. The website states that it may be worth including relevant experience gained from completing an extended project in your personal statement.

**Age and stage:** Oxford will assess a student's application on their ability, regardless of their age and they stress that no special consideration is given to younger candidates.

**14–19 Diplomas:** The Advanced Diploma in Engineering (Level 3) is considered an appropriate qualification for entry for engineering science courses at Oxford, but candidates must also obtain an A level in Physics and the new Level 3 Certificate in Mathematics for Engineering.

Diplomas in other subjects will only be suitable preparation for admission where candidates have opted for Additional Specialist Learning in two relevant A levels.

**Pre-U:** The Pre-U Diploma is considered to be a suitable qualification for candidates, and conditional offers are likely to vary between D2, D2, D3 and D3, D3, D3 depending on the subject. You will need to consult the course details given by the relevant faculties to find out the exact requirements for specific courses.

The University states that D2 is considered to be equivalent to an A\* grade at A level and D3 to an A grade and that candidates are allowed to take Pre-U Principal Subjects in place of A levels.

**YASS:** Oxford is happy to consider applications from students who have taken modules under the YASS (Young Applicants in Schools Scheme). YASS modules are offered by the Open University, and Oxford believes they can serve as useful preparation for study at university level. The Admissions Office suggests that candidates may wish to refer to these modules in their personal statement and discuss how they have benefitted from this extra study.

However, as most students who are taking YASS modules are also studying for A levels (or other equivalent qualifications), offers will usually be made on the basis of those A levels (or other equivalent qualifications) alone.

If you are studying Open University qualifications without additional qualifications, Oxford will be very pleased to consider an application from you. They state that they would generally expect strong candidates to have at least 120 points at level 1, in appropriate subjects.

**English Baccalaureate:** This is a relatively new qualification being introduced by the government and it is not expected to impact on a candidate's ability to make a competitive application. Oxford places far more importance on a candidate's ability to present a strong portfolio of GCSEs at A and A* grades.

**Vocational qualifications:** The University welcomes applications from students with vocational qualifications that are equivalent to A levels, but they may need additional academic qualifications to meet the admissions standard.

**International Baccalaureate:** The standard offer for International Baccalaureate students is 38–40 points, including core points, with 6s and 7s in the higher level.

**Scottish qualifications:** The current offer is for AAAAB or AAAAA in Scottish Highers with the addition of two or more Advanced Highers. Conditional offers require AAB if a student is able to take three Advanced Highers; if this is not possible, a student would be expected to achieve AA in two Advanced Highers, as well as an A grade in an additional Higher course taken in Sixth Year.

**US Qualifications:** Oxford will normally ask for SAT Reasoning Test scores of at least 700 in Critical Reading, Mathematics and the Writing Paper, or ACT with a score of at least 32 out of 36. It is also necessary to have achieved Grade 5 in three or more Advanced Placement tests in relevant subjects or SAT Subject Tests in three subjects at 700 or better.

**Other international qualifications:** For further details please see Chapter 10 on 'Non-standard applications'.

# 4 | The early stages of preparation

Choosing the right course is the most important decision you will have to make during the whole application process. It is primarily your enthusiasm for your subject that will be attractive to the admissions tutors and interviewers and, if you are accepted, your love for your subject will sustain you through all the hard work you will undoubtedly have to do. When considering which course to take and when preparing for interview, reading is another, and absolutely essential, form of preparation. You need to read widely and in depth. Knowing the school syllabus is not enough. You should be able to think and talk about ideas beyond the scope of school work and above the level of your peers.

## The importance of reading

Remember that the academics who teach at Oxford and Cambridge, and who interview prospective students, have dedicated their whole lives to their subject. They believe passionately in the importance of their research and expect you to do the same. If you have read around your subject this shows that you are dedicated and passionate and this will be very attractive to interviewers.

In addition, if you are accepted, the majority of your time as an undergraduate will be spent working. Whereas students on an essay-based course at UCL, for example, will be asked to write four 2,500-word essays over the course of a 10-week term, Oxbridge students are asked to write between 12 and 14 essays of the same length in the course of an eight-week term. Students who study science subjects at Oxbridge will have a large amount of contact time per week. These hours are made up of lab sessions, supervisions or tutorials, seminars and lectures that fill up most of the week and may run into your weekends. There is little time off, and most of it is taken up studying for assignments and essays. You need to be excited by this work and find the pressure enjoyable rather than a burden.

The method of working at Oxbridge is very different from school. Students who study humanities subjects (English literature, history and languages, for example) typically have very few hours of contact time in the week; perhaps six to eight hours of lectures and one hour-long seminar per week. However, they are expected to work as many hours as the scientists. This requires them to be independent in their study practice. Humanities students need to be dedicated, focused and able to follow through their own research without getting distracted. Like the scientists, therefore, humanities students need to show they are able to research independently.

Finally, in order to make the right choice it is important to gather as much information about a course and its content as possible. Prospectuses for Oxford and Cambridge give detailed course guides, including information on course content and A level requirements. In addition, Oxford makes individual prospectuses for each subject. Read this information and the criteria very carefully, making sure your qualifications fulfil the requirements specified.

If you want to be really thorough, contact the individual faculty secretaries at the university. Remember that, while the college administers the teaching, it is the faculty (i.e. the subject department within the university) that controls the syllabus. The faculty secretary will have much more detail on course content than is available in the prospectuses. Information about faculty addresses, including website addresses, is available in the prospectuses.

When you talk with the faculty secretary ask him or her for an up-to-date reading list for new undergraduates. This will list the books that students are expected to read before they come up to Cambridge or Oxford for the first time. If you dip into some of these books you will get an idea of the sort of information you will be tackling if you study the subject. In addition, if you have time to visit Cambridge or Oxford again, you could spend the afternoon in the university bookshop (Blackwell's in Oxford or Heffers in Cambridge). The staff at both bookshops will be very familiar with the texts used by undergraduates. Of course, if you know any current undergraduates at either university, discuss their work with them.

Collecting this information will boost your confidence and reassure you about your subject decision. Remember, in order to argue your case at interview, and to cope with the workload if you get a place, you must be deeply committed to your subject.

## Recommended reading

On the following pages is a list of suggested books and films that may help you to start your research. This list is not definitive and not officially endorsed by the Oxbridge faculties. As already stated, most faculties will have a recommended reading list on their websites and you should be familiar with this.

If you need further ideas, consult the list below. Don't feel you must read every book on this list, either. Dip into one or two to start with and see what particularly interests you. If your subject is not included here, or if you want to find out more, ask your teacher at your school or college for further guidance.

## Archaeology and anthropology

### Social anthropology

- Fox, K., *Watching the English*. London: Hodder & Stoughton, 2007.
- Monaghan, J. and Just, P., *Social and Cultural Anthropology: A Very Short Introduction*. Oxford: OUP, 2000.

### Biological anthropology

- Clack, T., *Ancestral Roots: Modern Living and Human Evolution*. Basingstoke: Palgrave Macmillan, 2008.
- Lewin, R., *Human Evolution: An Illustrated Introduction*. Oxford: Blackwell, 2005.

### Archaeology

- Gamble, C., *Archaeology: The Basics*. Abingdon: Routledge, 2000.
- Renfrew, C. and Bahn, P., *Archaeology: Theories, Methods and Practice*. London: Thames & Hudson, 2008.

### General books

- Barley, N., *The Innocent Anthropologist: Notes From A Mud Hut*. Long Grove, IL: Waveland, 2000.
- Carrithers, M., *Why Human Beings Have Cultures*. Oxford: OUP, 1992.
- Dunbar, R., *Gossip, Grooming and the Evolution of Language*. London: Faber, 1996.
- Fagan, B., *People of the Earth: An Introduction to World Prehistory*. London: Longman, 2004.
- Gosden, C., *Anthropology and Archaeology: A Changing Relationship*. Abingdon: Routledge, 1999.
- Harrison, G.A., *Human Biology: An Introduction to Human Evolution, Variation, Growth, and Adaptability*. Oxford: OUP, 1992.
- Haviland, W., *Cultural Anthropology*. London: Harcourt Brace, 2003.
- Hendry, J., *An Introduction to Social Anthropology: Other People's Worlds*. London: Macmillan, 1999.
- Keesing, R. and Strathern, A., *Cultural Anthropology: A Contemporary Perspective*. London: Harcourt Brace, 1998.
- Kuper, A., *The Chosen Primate: Human Nature and Cultural Diversity*. Cambridge, MA: Harvard University Press, 1996.
- Layton, R., *An Introduction to Theory in Anthropology*. Cambridge: CUP, 1998.

## Architecture

*Also look at the reading list for history of art.*

- Kenneth Frampton, *Modern Architecture, A Critical History.*
- Le Corbusier, *Towards a new Architecture.*
- Steen Eiler Rasmussen, *Experiencing Architecture.*
- John Summerson, *The Classical Language of Architecture.*
- Vitruvius, *The Ten Books on Architecture.*
- David Watkin, *The History of Western Architecture.*

## Art history

- H.H. Arnason and Peter Kalb, *History of Modern Art*, 5th edition, 2002.
- Michael Baxandall, *Painting and Experience in Fifteenth Century Italy: A Primer in the Social History of Pictorial Style*, 1972 and later edns.
- Mary Beard and John Henderson, *Classical Art From Greece to Rome*, 2001.
- John Berger, *Ways of Seeing*, 1972.
- John Boardman, ed., *Oxford History of Classical Art*, 1993.
- Michael Camille, *Gothic Art: Glorious Visions*, 1996.
- Craig Clunas, *Art in China*, 2nd edition, 2009.
- Thomas Crow, *The Rise of the Sixties: American and European Art in the Era of Dissent*, 1996.
- Jas Elsner, *Imperial Art and Christian Triumph: The Art of the Roman Empire, 100–450*, 1998.
- E.H. Gombrich, *The Story of Art*, 1950 and later edns.
- Michael Greenhalgh, *The Classical Tradition in Art*, 1978.
- Craig Harbison, *The Mirror of the Artist: Northern Renaissance Art in its Historical Context*, 1995.
- Francis Haskell, *History and Its Images: Art and the Interpretation of the Past*, 1993.
- Hugh Honour and John Fleming, *A World History of Art*, 7th edition, 2005.
- Geraldine A. Johnson, *Renaissance Art: A Very Short Introduction*, 2002.
- Linda Nochlin, *Women, Art and Power and other essays*, 1989.
- J.J. Pollitt, *Art and Experience in Classical Greece*, 1972.
- Steven J. Campbell and Michael W. Cole, *A new History of Italian Renaissance Art*, 2012.
- David Hockney, *Secret Techniques: Rediscovering the lost techniques of the Old Masters*, 2006.
- E. H. Gombrich, *Art and Illusion: A study in the psychology of pictorial representation*, 2002.

## Biological sciences (Oxford)

- Burton, R., *Biology by Numbers: An Encouragement to Quantitative Thinking*. Cambridge: CUP, 1998.
- Coyne, J., *Why Evolution is True*. Oxford: OUP, 2009.
- Chalmers, A.F., *What is This Thing Called Science?* Maidenhead: Open University Press, 1998.
- Collins, H.M. and Pinch, T., *The Golem: What You Should Know About Science*, 2nd edition. Cambridge: CUP, 1998.
- Freedman, D., Pisani, R. and Purves, R., *Statistics*, 3rd edition (although any edition would do). New York: W.W. Norton and Company Ltd., 1997.
- Southwood, R., *The Story of Life*. Oxford: OUP, 2003.

## Biochemistry (Oxford)

- Alberts, B. *et al.*, *Molecular Biology of the Cell*, 5th edition. Abingdon: Taylor & Francis, 2008.
- Alberts, B. *et al.*, *Essential Cell Biology*, 2nd edition. Abingdon: Taylor & Francis, 2003.
- Campbell, M. and Farrell, S., *Biochemistry*, 6th edition. Andover: Cengage Learning, 2008.
- Devlin, T., *Textbook of Biochemistry with Clinical Correlation*, 6th edition. Chichester: Wiley-Liss, 2005.
- Elliott, W. and Elliott, D., *Biochemistry and Molecular Biology*, 3rd edition. Oxford: OUP, 2004.
- Fox, M. and Whitesell, J., *Organic Chemistry*, 3rd edition. Sudbury, MA: Jones & Bartlett, 2004.
- Garret, R. and Grisham, C., *Biochemistry*, 3rd edition. Andover: Cengage Learning, 2005.
- Lewin, B. *et al.*, eds, *Cells*, 1st edition. Sudbury, MA: Jones & Bartlett, 2007.
- Lodish *et al.*, *Molecular Cell Biology*, 6th edition. New York, NY: W.H. Freeman.
- Stryer *et al.*, *Biochemistry*, 6th edition. New York, NY: W.H. Freeman, 2004.
- Sykes, P., *Guidebook to Mechanism in Organic Chemistry*, 6th edition. Englewood Cliffs, NJ: Prentice Hall, 1986.
- Voet, D., Voet J. and Pratt, C., *Fundamentals of Biochemistry*, 3rd edition. Chichester: John Wiley & Sons, 2008.

## Economics

- Dasgupta, P., *Economics: A Very Short Introduction*.
- Jacques, I., *Mathematics for Economics and Business*.
- Mankiw, N.G., and Taylor, M.P., *Macroeconomics*, European edition.

- *The Economist* (weekly).
- *Financial Times*.
- Varian, H., *Intermediate Microeconomics: A Modern Approach*.

## Microeconomics

- Begg, D.K.H., Fischer, S. and Dornbusch, R., *Economics*, latest edition. Maidenhead: McGraw-Hill, 2005.
- Dixit, A. and Skeath, S., *Games of Strategy*, 2nd edition. New York, NY: Norton, 2009.
- Morgan, W., Katz, M. and Rosen, S., *Microeconomics*, latest edition. Maidenhead: McGraw-Hill, 2005.
- Varian, H., *Intermediate Microeconomics*, latest edition. New York, NY: Norton, 2010.

## Macroeconomics

- Heilbroner, R., *The Worldly Philosophers*, latest edition. London: Penguin, 2000.
- Mankiw, N.G. and Taylor, M.P., *Macroeconomics*, European edition. New York, NY: W.H. Freeman, 2007.

## Quantitative methods in economics

- Aczel, A.D. and Sounderpandian, J., *Complete Business Statistics*, latest edition. Maidenhead: McGraw-Hill/Irwin, 2008.
- Bradley, T. and Patton, P., *Essential Mathematics for Economics and Business*, latest edition. Chichester: Wiley, 2008.
- Lind, D., Marchal, W. and Mason, R., *Statistical Techniques in Business and Economics*, latest edition. Maidenhead: McGraw-Hill/Irwin, 2009.
- Pemberton, M. and Rau, N., *Mathematics for Economists*, 2nd edition. Manchester: Manchester University Press, 2006.

## Political and sociological aspects of economics

- Donkin, R., *Blood, Sweat and Tears: the Evolution of Work*. London: Texere, 2001.
- Dunleavy, P. *et al.*, *Developments in British Politics*, latest edition. London: Macmillan, 2006.
- Easterlin, R., *The Reluctant Economist*. Cambridge: CUP, 2004.
- Hutton, W., *The World We're In*. London: Abacus, 2003.
- Toynbee, P., *Hard Work*. London: Bloomsbury, 2003.

## British economic history

- Broadberry, S. and Solomou, S., *Protectionism and Economic Revival: The British Inter-war Economy*. Cambridge: CUP, 2008.
- Floud, R. and Johnson, P., eds, *The Cambridge Economic History of Modern Britain* (three vols). Cambridge: CUP, 2004.
- Hudson, P., *The Industrial Revolution*. London: Hodder, 1992.
- Mathias, P., *The First Industrial Nation*. Abingdon: Routledge, 2001.

## UK, European and world history

- Clarke, P., *Hope and Glory*. London: Penguin, 2004.
- Diamond, J., *Guns, Germs and Steel*. London: Vintage, 2005.
- Hobsbawm, E., *Age of Extremes: the Short Twentieth Century 1914–1991*, London: Abacus, 1995.
- Judt, T., *PostWar*. London: Vintage, 2010.
- Mazower, M., *Dark Continent: Europe's Twentieth Century*. London: Penguin, 2008.
- Landes, D.S, *The Wealth and Poverty of Nations: Why Are Some So Rich and Others So Poor?*. New York, NY: Norton, 1999.
- Johnston, R. *et al.*, eds, *The Dictionary of Human Geography*, 4th edition. Chichester: Blackwell, 2000.
- Thomas, D. and Goudie, A., eds, *The Dictionary of Physical Geography*, 3rd edition. Chichester: Blackwell, 2000.

## English

*Your personal statement should identify your knowledge and appreciation of authors outside those of the English A level syllabus. It is sensible also to display an interest in different genres and periods: a student who only referred to twentieth century American literary texts would not be impressing overly. You should not simply be reeling names off but explaining why your chosen authors mean so much to you and if you display an interest in the work of an author it is only sensible to have read more than one work by him/her and to have considered the cultural context in which they operated.*

- Peter Barry, *Beginning Theory: An Introduction to Literary and Cultural Theory.*
- Jonathan Bate, *The Soul of the Age: Life, Mind and World of William Shakespeare.*
- Jonathan Culler, *Literary Theory: A Very Short Introduction.*
- Jonathan Culler, *On Deconstruction: Theory and Criticism after Structuralism.*
- Jonathan Culler, *Structuralist Poetics.*
- David Daiches, *Critical Approaches to English Literature.*
- Terry Eagleton, *Philosophy after Objectivity.*
- Wilfred L. Guerin et al, *A Handbook of Approaches to Literature.*
- Chris Hopkins, *Thinking About Texts: An Introduction to English Studies.*
- John Kerrigan, *Revenge Tragedy: From Aeschylus to Armageddon.*
- A.D. Nuttall, *Why Does Tragedy Give Pleasure?*
- A.D. Nutall, *A New Mimesis.*

## History

*The key piece of advice for would-be Oxbridge historians is to ensure that you have read widely around your A level topics. You need to show an awareness of recent historical debate and to understand different interpretations of the same events. The books listed below either deal with historiography or are particularly well written and deserve attention.*

- Tim Blanning, *Pursuit of Glory.*
- Michael Burleigh, *Moral Combat.*
- C. Carpenter, *The Wars of the Roses.*
- David Cannadine, *In Churchill's Shadow.*
- C.S.L. Davies, *Peace, Print and Protestantism 1450–1558.*
- Geoffrey Elton, *The Practice of History.*
- Richard J Evans, *In Defence of History.*
- J. Guy, *Tudor England.*
- E. Hallam, *Chronicles of the Age of Chivalry and Chronicles of the Wars of the Roses.*
- M.H. Keen, *England in the Later Middle Ages.*
- D.M. Loades, *Politics and the Nation 1450–1660.*
- Mark Mazower, *Dark Continent: Europe's Twentieth Century.*
- Blair Worden, *Roundhead Reputations.*

### 370-900

- J. Herrin, *The Formation of Christendom.*
- R. Hodges, D. Whitehouse, *Mohammed, Charlemagne and the Origins of Europe.*
- J. Nelson, *Charles the Bald.*
- M. Whitlow, *The Making of Orthodox Byzantium, 600–1025.*

### 1000-1300

- R. Bartlett, *The Making of Europe: Conquest, Colonization and Cultural Change, 950–1350.*
- G. Holmes, ed., *The Oxford Illustrated History of Medieval Europe.*
- R.W. Southern, *The Making of the Middle Ages.*

### 1400-1650

- A.G. Dickens, *Reformation and Society in Sixteenth Century Europe* and *The Counter Reformation.*
- G. Parker, *Europe in Crisis 1598–1648.*

### 1815-1914

- E.J. Hobsbawm, *The Age of Revolution 1789–1848*, *The Age of Capital 1848–1875*, and *The Age of Empire 1878–1914.*

## Law

- Catherine Appleton, *Life after Life Imprisonment.*
- Marcel Berlins and Clare Dyer, *The Law Machine.*

- Lord Denning, *The Discipline of Law*.
- J.A.G. Griffith, *The Politics of the Judiciary*.
- Trevor Grove, *The Juryman's Tale*.
- Trevor Grove, *The Magistrate's Tale*.
- James A. Holland and Julian S. Webb, *Learning Legal Rules*.
- Michael J. Klarman, *Brown v. Board of Education and the Civil Rights Movement*.
- Nick McBride, *Letters to a Law Student*.
- Ian McLeod, *Legal Method*.
- John Pritchard, *The New Penguin Guide to the Law*.
- John Vidal, *McLibel: Burger, Culture on Trial*.
- Glanville Williams, *Learning the Law*. (This is a popular introductory book. It will not give you any specific, substantive legal knowledge – but it will provide you with useful information ranging from how to read cases to what the abbreviations mean.)
- Jeremy Waldron, *The Law*.

## Linguistics

- Akmajian, A., *Linguistics: An Introduction to Language and Communication*. Cambridge, MA: MIT Press, 2001.
- Atkinson, M. *et al.*, *Foundations of General Linguistics*. London: Unwin Hyman, 1988.
- Fromkin, V. *et al.*, *An Introduction to Language*. Boston, MA: Thomson/Heinle, 2003.
- Newmeyer, F.J., ed., *Linguistics: The Cambridge Survey*. Cambridge: CUP, 1998.
- Radford, A., *Linguistics: An Introduction*. Cambridge: CUP, 1999.

## Management

- Dixit, A. and Nalebuff, B., *Thinking Strategically: The Competitive Edge in Business, Politics, and Everyday Life*. New York, NY: W.W. Norton and Co, 1991.
- Handy, C., *Understanding Organisations*, 4th edition. London: Penguin, 1993.
- Pfeffer, J., *The Human Equation: Building Profits by Putting People First*. Watertown, MA: Harvard Business School Press, 1998.
- Pfeffer, J. and Sutton, R., *Hard Facts, Dangerous Half-Truths and Total Nonsense: Profiting From Evidence-Based Management*. Boston, MA: Harvard Business School Press, 2006.
- Tedlow, R., *New and Improved: The Story of Mass Marketing in America*, Maidenhead: McGraw-Hill, 1996.
- McCraw, T.K., *Creating Modern Capitalism: How Entrepreneurs, Companies, and Countries Triumphed in Three Industrial Revolutions*. Watertown, MA: Harvard Business School Press, 1998.

## Medicine

- Isaac Asimov, *New Guide to Science*.
- Bill Bryson, *A Short History of Nearly Everything*.
- Calvin W.H. and Ojemann G., *Conversations with Neil's Brain*.
- Susan Greenfield, *The Human Brain: A Guided Tour*.
- Diarmuid Jeffreys, *Aspirin*.
- Dr Melvin Konner, *The Trouble with Medicine*.
- P.B. Medawar, *Advice to a Young Scientist*.
- Denis Noble, *The Music of Life*.
- Sherwin Nuland, *How We Die*.
- Sherwin Nuland, *How We Live*.
- Jo Revill, *Everything You Need to Know about Bird Flu*.
- Matt Ridley, *Genome*.
- Oliver Sacks, *The Man Who Mistook His Wife For a Hat*.
- David Seedhouse and Lisetta Lovett, *Practical Medical Ethics*.
- Lewis Thomas, *The Youngest Science*.
- James Watson, *DNA: The Secret of Life*.
- D.J. Weatherall, *Science and the Quiet Art*.
- Dr David Wilham, *Body Story*.

---

### Podcasts

Oxford Podcasts:
http://podcasts.ox.ac.uk
www.bbc.co.uk/sn

Radio 4 podcasts index:
www.bbc.co.uk/radio4/programmes/genres/factual/scienceand
nature

---

## Modern languages

### French: reading

- Albert Camus, *La Chute*.
- Marie Cardinal, *La Cié sur la Porte*.
- Gustave Flaubert, *Trois Contes*.
- André Gide, *La Porte étroite*.
- Molière, *Le Misanthrope*.
- Marcel Proust, *Sur la Lecture*.
- La Rochefoucauld, *Maximes*.
- Voltaire, *Candide* or *Micromegas* (short story).

### French: films

- *Francois Truffaut, Robert Bresson, André Téchiné, Eric Rohmer and Louis Malle are important figures in French cinema. Read the following texts if possible:*

- Bresson, *Notes Sur le Cinématographe*.
- Truffaut, *Les Films de Ma Vie*.

## German: reading

- Heinrich Böll, *Die Verlorene Ehre der Katharina Blum*.
- Bertolt Brecht, *Kaukasischer Kreidekreis*; *Mutter Courage*.
- Friedrich Dürrenmatt, *Die Physiker*; *Der Besuch der alten Dame*.
- Max Frisch, *Andorra*.
- Gunther Grass, *Die Blechtrommel*; *Katz und Maus*.
- Franz Kafka, *Die Verwandlung*; *Sämtliche Erzählungen*.
- Thomas Mann, *Tonio Kröger*; *Der Tod in Venedig*.
- Bernhard Schlink, *Der Vorleser*.
- Patrick Süskind, *Das Parfum*; *Die Taube*.

## German: art

*Taschen books are readily available and cheap. Read in English or German. Books are available on the following subjects:*

- Expressionism
- Bauhaus
- Wiener Werkstätte.

## German: films

Films about the Second World War:

- *Das Boot.*
- *Europa, Europa.*
- *Die Faelscher.*
- *Heimat.*
- *Sophie Scholl.*
- *Der Untergang.*

Films about the former East Germany:

- *Goodbye Lenin!*
- *Der Himmel über Berlin.*
- *Leben der Anderen.*
- *Sonnenallee.*
- *Der Tunnel.*

## Italian: reading

- Italo Calvino, *Se una notte d'inverno un viaggiatore*.
- Natalia Ginzburg, *Lessico famigliare*.
- Tomasi di Lampedusa, *Il gattopardo*.
- Primo Levi, *Se questo è un uomo*.
- Luigi Pirandello, *Sei personaggi in cerca d'autore*.
- Leonardo Sciascia, *A ciascuno il suo*.
- Italo Svevo, *La coscienza di Zeno*.

## Russian: reading

- Anna Akhmatova, *Requiem*.
- Iosif Brodsky, *Collected Poems in English 1972–1999*.
- Mikhail Bulgakov, *The Master and Margarita*.
- Ivan Bunin, *Life of Arseniev*.
- Anton Chekhov, *Uncle Vanya*.
- Fyodor Dostoevsky, *The Brothers Karamazov*.
- Nikolai Gogol, *Taras Bulba*.
- Mikhail Lermontov, *A Hero of our Time*.
- Boris Pasternak, *Doctor Zhivago*.
- Alexander Pushkin, *Eugene Onegin*.
- Aleksandr Solzhenitsyn, *One Day in the Life of Ivan Denisovich*.
- Leo Tolstoy, *Anna Karenina*.
- Ivan Turgenev, *A Month in the Country*.

## Spanish: reading

- *Lazarillo de Tormes*.
- Leopoldo Alas, *La Regenta*.
- Pedro Calderón de la Barca, *La Vida es Sueño*.
- Pio Baroja, *El árbol de la Ciencia*.
- Camilo José Cela, *La Familia de Pascual Duarte*; *La Colmena*.
- Miguel de Cervantes, *El Quijote*.
- Julio Cortázar, *Rayuela*.
- Miguel Delibes, *Cinco Horas con Mario*.
- Rafael Sánchez Ferlosio, *El Jarama*.
- Carmen Martin Gaite, *Lo Raro es Vivir*.
- Juan Goytisolo, *Señas de Identidad*.
- Mario Vargas Llosa, *Ta Tia Julia*.
- Federico García Lorca, *Poeta en Nueva York*; *La Casa de Bernarda Alba*.
- Carlos Marcial, *El Surrealismo y Cuatro Poetas de la Generación del 27: (Ensayo Sobre Extensión y Límites Del Surrealismo en la Generación Del 27)*.
- Javier Marías, *Corazón Tan Blanco*.
- Gabriel Garcia Márquez, *Cien Años de Soledad*.
- Luis Martin-Santos, *Tiempo de Silencio*.
- Ana María Matute, *Olvidado Rey Gudú*.
- Eduardo Mendoza, *La Ciudad de los Prodigios*.
- Pablo Neruda, *Confieso Que he Vivido*.
- Fernando de Rojas, *La Celestina*.
- Miguel de Unamuno, *La Tía Tula*.

## Spanish: films

- Pedro Almodóvar, *Todo Sobre mi Madre*.
- Jaime Chávarri, *Las Bicicletas son Para el Verano*.
- Víctor Erice, *El Espíritu de la Colmena*.

- Alejandro González Iñárritu, *Amores Perros*; *La Caza*.
- Carlos Saura, *Cría Cuervos*; *Elisa, Vida Mía*.

## Music

*In addition to reading you should become familiar with the Dover scores of string quartets and symphonies by Haydn, Mozart, and Beethoven. Aim to get to know several quartets and symphonies by all three composers.*

- Aldwell, E. and Schachter, C., *Harmony and Voice Leading*, 3rd edition. Belmont, CA: Wadsworth Publishing Co, 2002.
- Bohlman, P., *World Music: A Very Short Introduction*. Oxford: OUP, 2002.
- Clayton, M., Herbert, T. and Middleton, R., eds, *The Cultural Study of Music: A Critical Introduction*. Abingdon: Routledge, 2003.
- Caplin, W.E., *Classical Form: A Theory of Formal Functions for the Instrumental Music of Haydn, Mozart, and Beethoven*. Oxford: OUP, 1998. (This will be invaluable not only for your Analysis studies but also for your understanding of classical-period harmony.)
- Cook, N., *A Guide to Musical Analysis*. Oxford: OUP, 1994.
- Cook, N., *Music: A Very Short Introduction*. Oxford: OUP, 2000.
- Ledbetter, D., ed., *Continuo Playing According to Handel*. Wotton-Under-Edge: Clarendon Press, 1990.
- Morris, R.O. and Ferguson, H., *Preparatory Exercises in Score Reading*. Oxford: OUP, 1931.
- Parker, R., ed., *The Oxford Illustrated History of Opera*. Oxford: OUP, 1994.
- *The New Harvard Dictionary of Music*, Cambridge, MA: Harvard University Press, 1986; or *The Grove Concise Dictionary of Music*. London: Macmillan, 1988. (Both are useful reference books.)

### Harmony and counterpoint

*Play and study the following:*

- *The Chorale Harmonisations of J.S. Bach*. Recommended edition: Breitkopf and Härtel, ed. B.F. Richter; less good but adequate: Chappell, ed. Albert Riemenschneider.
- *Fugal Expositions by J.S. Bach in the Well-tempered Clavier (the '48')*. Recommended edition: Associated Board, ed. Richard Jones.
- *Schubert Lieder*. Recommended edition: Dover (either *Schubert's Songs to Texts* by Goethe or *Complete Song Cycles*). The Lieder of Beethoven, Mendelssohn, and Schumann are also recommended for your attention.
- Renaissance polyphony. Listen to some of the many fine recordings of the music of Palestrina and his contemporaries (the Gimell and Hyperion labels are a rich source).

## Natural science (Cambridge)

*Biology of cells*

- Alberts, B. *et al..*, *Molecular Biology of the Cell.* Abingdon: Taylor & Francis, 2008.

*Computer science*

- Dewdney, A.K., *The New Turing Omnibus.* Computer Sciences Press, 1993 (reprinted 2001, Henry Holt).
- Körner, Tom W., *The Pleasures of Counting.* Cambridge: CUP, 1996.

*Evolution and behaviour*

- Barton, N. *et al.*, *Evolution.* Woodbury, NY: Cold Spring Harbour Lab. Press, 2007.
- Dawkins, R., *The Ancestor's Tale: A Pilgrimage to the Dawn of Life.* London: Weidenfeld & Nicolson, 2004.

*Chemistry*

- Boyd, Robert N. and Morrison, Robert T., *Organic Chemistry.* Upper Saddle River, NJ: 1992.
- Cotton, F. Albert *et al.*, *Advanced Inorganic Chemistry.* Chichester: Wiley, 1999.
- Atkins, Peter and Paula, Julio de, *Atkins' Physical Chemistry.* Oxford: OUP, 2009.

*Geology (earth sciences)*

- Benton, M.J., *When Life Nearly Died.* London: Thames & Hudson, 2005.
- Ince, M., *Rough Guide to the Earth.* London: Rough Guides/ Penguin, 2007.

*Materials science*

- Ball, P., *Made to Measure: New Materials for the 21st Century.* Princeton, NJ: Princeton University Press.
- Cotterill, R.M.J., *The Material World.* Cambridge: CUP, 2008.
- Gordon, J.E., *New Science of Strong Materials.* London: Penguin, 1991.

*Physiology of organisms*

- King, J., *Reaching for the Sun.* Cambridge: CUP, 1997.
- Alberts, B. *et al.*, *Molecular Biology of the Cell.* Abingdon: Taylor & Francis, 2008.
- Widmaier, E.P., *Why Geese Don't Get Obese (And We Do).* New York, NY: WH Freeman, 2000.

## Mathematics

- Gower, T., *Mathematics: A Very Short Introduction.* Oxford: OUP, 2002.
- Körner, Tom W., *The Pleasures of Counting.* Cambridge: CUP, 1996.
- Sivia, D.S. and Rawlings, S.G., *Foundations of Science Mathematics* Oxford: OUP, 1999.

## Elementary mathematics

- Foster, P.C., *Easy Mathematics for Biologists.* Abingdon: CRC, 1999.
- Huff, D., *How to Lie with Statistics.* London: Penguin, 1991.
- Rowntree, D., *Statistics Without Tears – an Introduction for Non-mathematicians.* London: Penguin, 2000.

# Philosophy

- Alexander, H.G., *The Leibniz–Clarke Correspondence.*
- Ayer, A.J., *The Central Questions of Philosophy.*
- Blackburn, S., *The Big Questions.*
- Bryson, N., *Vision and Painting.*
- Dancy, J., *An Introduction to Contemporary Epistemology.*
- Descartes, R., *Discourse on the Method* (many translations).
- Hodges, W., *Logic.*
- Honderich, T., *The Oxford Companion to Philosophy.*
- Hospers, J., *An Introduction to Philosophical Analysis.*
- Levinson. J., *The Oxford Handbook of Aesthetics.*
- Nagel, T., *What does it all mean?.*
- O'Hear, A., *What Philosophy Is: An Introduction to Contemporary Philosophy.*
- Runciman, W.G., *Great Books, Bad Arguments.*
- Shand, J., *Philosophy and Philosophers.*
- Warburton, N., *Philosophy: The Classics.*

# Physics

- John P. Cullerne and Anton Machacek, *The Language of Physics.*
- Richard P Feynman, *Six Easy Pieces.*
- Richard P Feynman, *Six Not So Easy Pieces.*

For those with an interest in engineering:

- J. E. Gordon, *Structures, or Why Things Don't Fall Down.*
- J. E. Gordon, *The New Science of Strong Materials.*
- Henry Petroski, *Invention by Design.*

## Politics

- Elliott, F. and Hanning, J., *Cameron*. London: Harper Collins, 2012.
- Heffernan, R. (ed.) *et al.*, *Developments in British Politics 9*. Basingstoke: Palgrave Macmillan, 2011.
- McCormick, J., *European Union Politics*. Basingstoke: Palgrave Macmillan, 2011.
- McCormick, J., *Contemporary Britain*, Basingstoke: Palgrave Macmillan, 2012.
- Vieira, M.B. and Runciman, D., *Representation*. Cambridge: Polity Press, 2008.

## Psychology

- Rita Carter, *Mapping the Mind*.
- Hugh Coolican, *Introduction to Research Methods and Statistics in Psychology*.
- Sigmund Freud, *The Psychopathology of Everyday Life*.
- Daniel Goleman, *Emotional Intelligence*.
- Richard D. Gross, *Psychology: The Science of Mind and Behaviour*.
- Nicky Hayes, *Foundations of Psychology: Introductory Text*.
- Miles Hewstone, Frank Fincham and Jonathan Foster, *Psychology; British Psychology*.
- Michael Hogg and Graham Vaughan, *Social Psychology: An Introduction*.
- Allan Pease, *Body Language*.
- H. Rudolf Schaffer, *Introducing Child Psychology; Concepts in Developmental Psychology*.
- Robert Winston, *The Human Mind*.

> *The Psychologist*, a monthly publication of the British Psychological Society, has back issues freely available on its archive at www.thepsychologist.org.uk

## Sociology

- Alexander, J.C. and Thompson, K., *A Contemporary Introduction to Sociology: Culture and Society in Transition*. London/Boulder, CO: Paradigm Publishers, 2008.
- Crompton, R., *Class and Stratification*, 3rd edition. Cambridge: Polity Press, 2008.
- Giddens, A., *Sociology*, 6th edition. Cambridge: Polity Press, 2009.
- Sennett, R., *The Culture of the New Capitalism*. London: Yale University Press, 2006.

## Statistics

- Graham, A., *Teach Yourself Statistics*. Maidenhead: McGraw-Hill, 2008.
- Huff, D., *How to Lie with Statistics*. London: Penguin, 1991.
- Rowntree, D., *Statistics Without Tears – an Introduction for Non-mathematicians*. London: Penguin, 2000.

## Theology

### General

- Karen Armstrong, *The Case for God*
- Richard Dawkins, *The Blind Watchmaker*
- Richard Dawkins, *The God Delusion*
- Alistair McGrath, *The Dawkins Delusion*
- Philip Pullman, *His Dark Materials*

### Biblical

- Alice Ogden Bellis, *Helpmates, Harlots and Heroes*
- David Clines, *The theme of the Pentateuch*
- Michael Lambek (ed.), *A Reader in the Anthropology of Religion*
- John Painter, *The Quest for the Messiah*

### History and doctrine

- St Augustine, *City of God*
- St Augustine, *The Confessions*
- Eamon Duffy, *The Stripping of the Altars*
- Colin E. Gunton, *The One, the Three and the Many*
- Alistair McGrath, *Reformation Thought*
- Alistair McGrath, *Modern Christian Thought*

## Further resources

In addition to the suggestions above, remember to:

- read around your subject in the press
- search for podcasts and videos
- check out blogs and online articles.

# 5 | Choosing your university and college

So you've decided that you want to apply. You're studying the right A levels, you are predicted or already have the appropriate grades and you've been reading around your subject. What next?

As an undergraduate, you may only apply to one of either Oxford or Cambridge, and therefore, you need to decide which. You should try and make an educated choice; ideally do your research and visit both, have a look round the various colleges and university buildings and drink in the atmosphere. Talk to friends who are currently at Oxbridge and teachers who have been there. You also need to understand the courses each university offers; for example, Cambridge offers Natural Sciences in place of Physics, Chemistry or Biology; Politics, Philosophy and Economics (PPE) is unique to Oxford as is Social and Political Sciences to Cambridge.

## Which university?

There are several reasons to choose one university over the other but the most important aspect to consider is whether it offers you the right course. Oxford and Cambridge agree that the most important decision a prospective applicant has to make is the degree they wish to study, not which university they want to apply to. Both universities are committed to recruiting the most talented students regardless of their background and both are world class in teaching and research in both arts and science subjects.

### First, choose your course

It is essential to check that the university you prefer teaches the subject you wish to study. There are various subjects that Oxford offers which Cambridge does not and vice versa.

Subjects you can study at **Cambridge** but not at Oxford include:

- architecture
- architecture and geography

- Asian and Middle Eastern studies
- economics (as a stand-alone subject; at Oxford you do a combined course of economics and management)
- education studies
- land economy
- the languages Dutch, Anglo-Saxon, Norse and Celtic
- management studies (as a stand-alone subject; at Oxford you do a combined course of economics and management)
- natural sciences (at Oxford all the sciences are offered but not in the same combination)
- philosophy (as a stand-alone subject; at Oxford you do a combined course such as philosophy, politics and economics or physics and philosophy)
- social and political science (SPS)
- veterinary medicine.

Subjects you can study at **Oxford** but not at Cambridge include:

- the languages Sanskrit and Czech with Slovak
- Oriental studies
- philosophy, politics and economics (PPE)
- psychology and philosophy
- separate sciences (although you may have to take modules in other science subjects as well).

Subjects you can study at both universities include:

- archaeology and anthropology
- classics
- computer science
- engineering
- English literature and language
- geography
- history
- human sciences
- law
- modern and medieval languages
- music
- theology and religious studies.

It is important to note that, although many subjects are the same, their components may differ between the two universities and you should take time to compare the courses in detail.

For more information go to the websites listed below.

- Cambridge: www.cam.ac.uk/admissions/undergraduate/courses.
- Oxford: www.admissions.ox.ac.uk/courses.

## Course flexibility

At Oxford, most subjects include compulsory courses for the first year, and then give students the opportunity to choose options in subsequent years. At Cambridge, courses cover the subject very broadly in the initial years and then become more specialised within a wide range of options in the later years.

Comparing the Tripos system at Cambridge with the two-part system at Oxford can be another way to help you to decide which university is better suited to you. One of the great attractions of Cambridge is the flexibility of its Tripos system (the name Tripos is said to have been derived from the three-legged stool that undergraduates in the Middle Ages sat on for their oral examinations).

Each course, or Tripos, is usually divided into two parts: Part I and Part II. After each part there is an exam that counts towards your final undergraduate mark. A Part I can take one year (in economics, for example) or two years (in English). A two-year Part I is divided into Part IA and Part IB. Once you have completed Part I (A and B), you have the option of continuing to specialise in the same subject, or swapping to a related but different subject for Part II.

In theory, this gives students quite a bit of flexibility, and there have been students who have studied three different but related subjects during the course of their three years at Cambridge and come out with a First Class degree. In reality, however, you should not go to interview thinking that you will be able to change courses easily. Admissions tutors, particularly those interviewing for humanities, arts and social sciences, will see this as a sign that a student is not committed to their subject, and give the place to someone who is. If students want to change subject when they get to Cambridge they have to work very hard at convincing their current Director of Studies (DOS) that they want to change for the right reasons. Then students have to convince the DOS in their new subject to take them on.

On the other hand, there are subjects where elongated undergraduate degrees are encouraged. Natural sciences and mathematics students have the option of adding a Part III, while engineering students take Parts IA, IB, IIA and IIB over four years, leading ultimately to the award of MEng.

The system works slightly differently at Oxford. As at Cambridge, students have to pass exams in two parts. However, students do not have to take examinations at the end of each year, as is the case in many Cambridge courses. The Preliminary Examinations (or 'Prelims') are taken at the end of the first year (apart for a few exceptions) and the Final Examinations ('Finals') are taken at the end of the third year. Most arts and social science undergraduates at Oxford University do not take exams in their second year; maths and science students take exams at the end of each year.

In general there are more courses at Oxford which are designed to take four years. The Joint Honours courses of Mathematics and Philosophy and Physics and Philosophy, as well as Classics, take four years. Mathematics itself, Physics and Earth Sciences can take either three or four years (your choice), but in the case of Molecular and Cellular Biochemistry, Chemistry, Engineering and Metallurgy, students are normally expected to progress to the fourth research-based year leading to the award of a master's degree.

You should research the similarities and differences that apply to your particular subject choice carefully, and then be prepared to discuss your discoveries when it comes to the interview stage.

---

**Case study: Jonathan, Sidney Sussex College, Cambridge**

I was always good at science subjects at school, probably because I have a mathematical mind and I always hated writing essays! I got A*s in Maths, Chemistry, Physics and Biology so I chose to study those subjects at A level. My teachers were really encouraging, too, and they suggested that I might be good enough to apply to Oxford or Cambridge.

When I got into my A2 year and had to submit my UCAS form, I wasn't sure which university to apply to, as no one in my family and none of my friends had ever applied before. I went online to read about the science courses at both universities. Oxford offers physics, biology and chemistry as separate degree subjects, for instance, but Cambridge do this brilliant course called Natural Sciences that seemed to me to combine the best of all worlds.

The course is split broadly into biological and physical sciences, but in first year you can select subjects from both areas and you don't need to decide what your specialist subjects will be until the start of second year.

This year I have had to do a maths option, which involves fairly advanced Maths to Quantitative Biology. You have to choose three modules out of Biology of Cells, Chemistry, Computer Science, Earth Sciences, Evolution and Behaviour, Material Sciences, Physics and Physiology of Organisms. I will probably choose to do all physical or all biological subjects but a lot of students do a mix, which I suppose keeps their options open.

I am enjoying my time at Cambridge very much; I have to work extremely hard to cope with my academic work but there is enough downtime to play rugby and spend time with friends. You won't

---

believe how good the teaching is here; my tutors are experts in their field and yet they are down to earth and helpful. The other natural science students are great, too, and although it sounds a bit nerdy to say that we enjoy discussing our subject late into the night, it really does happen sometimes!

## Other factors to consider

### The location

Oxford is located about 100km (62 miles) north-west of London, with excellent links to the capital and the rest of the country by car, coach and train. It is a lively, medium-sized city with a total student population of over 40,000 (including students at both Oxford and Oxford Brookes). Most university and college buildings are located in the centre and are easily reached on foot or by bike.

Cambridge lies 88.5km (55 miles) north of London, off the M11 motor-way and is a 45-minute journey by train from the capital. Stansted Airport is 48km (30 miles) away. The city has also become the centre of the hi-tech 'Silicon Fen' industries. It is much smaller than Oxford and this can make Cambridge feel claustrophobic for some, but there are plenty of open, green spaces in this undeniably beautiful place.

### The student mix

Oxford has a 55% male, 45% female (undergraduates 53% male, 47% female) ratio. All students: 64% home, 36% overseas (undergraduates 86% home, 14% overseas). State school intake (undergraduates): 53.9%.

Cambridge's profile is very similar: 52% male, 48% female. State school intake (undergraduates): 59%. Of 17,000 students at Cambridge, 1,000 are international.

### Teaching

Teaching methods are very similar at both universities, as students will attend lectures, classes and laboratory work, as appropriate for their course. Unlike many other universities, students at Oxford and Cambridge also benefit from one-to-one teaching from world experts in their field. The only difference is in the name: Oxford refers to these sessions as 'tutorials' while Cambridge calls them 'supervisions'.

### Assessment

Students at Oxford and Cambridge are assessed informally throughout their course by producing work for their tutors/supervisors for weekly tutorials/supervisions. Formal assessment is almost entirely based on examinations, although in the final year of many courses one examina-tion paper can be replaced with a dissertation.

At Oxford the final degree classification result is usually based on the examinations taken at the end of the final year. Cambridge students, in contrast, are assessed through examinations in more than one year of their courses.

### Research standards

Oxford has more world-leading academics than any other UK university (rated 4* in the 2008 national Research Assessment Exercise). It has consistently boasted the highest research income from external sponsors of any UK university, and receives the highest level of quality research funding from HEFCE.

Cambridge is equally blessed financially, and performance league tables consistently place Cambridge among the world's top-ranking institutions.

### Availability of part-time work

Oxford offers opportunities for a limited amount of paid work within college, for which you may need your tutor's permission, and colleges sometimes offer employment during the summer conference season. The University Careers Service facilitates summer internship and work opportunities through the Oxford University International Internship Programme and on-campus employer events and fairs.

Cambridge states that since the university terms are short and highly demanding on students' time and intellectual capabilities, it strongly discourages taking on part-time work. However, as a Cambridge undergraduate, you will find it relatively easy to procure internships and holiday work if you are prepared to put enough effort into researching and applying.

## Which college?

Your next decision is which college to choose. Many students are thrown into a complete quandary about this and at first sight it seems hard to know how to decide. Your college will be the centre of your academic and social life and it is worth putting a bit of thought into why you might prefer one over another.

Oxford and Cambridge colleges are independent, self-governing communities of academics, students and staff. The collegiate system gives students and academics the benefits of belonging to both a large, internationally renowned institution and to a smaller, interdisciplinary, academic college community. Colleges and halls enable leading academics and students across subjects and year groups and from different cultures and countries to work and socialise together. This system gives you the opportunity to discuss your work in college tutorials and seminars, over meals in the dining hall or in your college accommodation late into the evening, and it will provide you with the chance to establish a new circle of friends quickly, and to access a range of varied social and sporting activities.

Your college will have a Senior Tutor whose role includes general oversight of all undergraduate members of the college, although your academic studies will be directed by your department or faculty. The relatively small number of students at each college allows for close and supportive personal attention to be given to the induction, academic development and welfare of individual students. Each student has a College Adviser, who is a member of the college's academic staff, and will be able to offer support and advice.

## Open application

If you cannot decide which college to apply to, it is possible to make an open application. An open application is where you do not choose a college; instead, you are assigned to one by the Admissions Board. Allocation is often to 'less popular' colleges; this does not make them bad colleges, simply colleges which have fewer applicants than others in the current cycle of applications. Both universities stress that making an open application in no way disadvantages you.

You may decide to make an open application if you really don't mind what your college life will be like. However, college life is such a great and unique aspect of Oxbridge that it's well worth at least putting some thought into it. Making an open application will not disadvantage you, so don't be afraid to take this route if you really feel it is best for you.

If you decide not to make an open application, the next step is to narrow down the list of 31 colleges at Cambridge and 38 colleges (and six permanent private halls) at Oxford to make your personal shortlist from which you will make your final choice.

## How do I choose a college that is right for me?

You might consider any or all of the following factors when making your decision:

### Does it offer the right course?

Some colleges will have a great reputation for certain courses (such as Balliol for PPE, for instance) and some will not offer every course offered by the universities.

To find out which colleges offer your course, you can see a comprehensive list at www.oxbridgecolleges.com.

### Do you want to be with a certain type of student?

A minority of colleges admit only certain groups of students, so if you want to be in a women-only college or with more mature or graduate students your options are limited.

**Women only:** Murray Edwards (formerly New Hall), Newnham, Lucy Cavendish at Cambridge.

**Mature students (over 21 at matriculation) only:** Clare Hall, Darwin, Hughes Hall, Lucy Cavendish, St Edmund's, Wolfson at Cambridge.

**Graduates only:** Clare Hall, Darwin at Cambridge; Green Templeton, Kellogg, Harris Linacre, Nuffield, St Anthony's, St Cross and Wolfson at Oxford.

### Does it have the right character?

There's no question that each college has its distinct character, whether it is highly academic, sporty or literary. Certainly, there is an element of 'horses for courses', if you'll pardon the pun. Being with like-minded students may make you work harder but if you're the kind of person that would rather come out with a 2.i and have captained a sports team or run student societies than strive for a First, then you may want to pick somewhere that will be sympathetic to your aspirations.

Every year, Oxford publishes the Norrington Table and Cambridge the Tompkins Table (see Appendix 3) that ranks the colleges in order of the number of First Class degrees achieved by their students in their final exams and this may give you some indication of the colleges' academic prowess. But beware of placing too much importance on this; colleges go up and down the tables at an alarming rate and those at the top of the tables one year may find themselves halfway down the next.

### What are the admissions criteria?

The colleges all have different admissions criteria for the subjects they offer. In addition to the information provided by your UCAS application, some colleges will request some sample work and some will require candidates to sit a test at interview. You need to read the admission criteria for your course very carefully and this may help you decide. You might find there are admissions criteria you aren't comfortable with or even highlight colleges whose criteria particularly appeal to you.

### Is the location convenient?

It's definitely worth locating your faculty buildings and lecture halls and seeing which colleges are nearby. This may sound faintly ridiculous when most of the colleges are located quite centrally but you will be delighted to be able to fall out of bed and be at your lecture within 10 minutes of waking up after a hard night of working or playing. Bear in mind a lot of people cycle around Oxford and Cambridge, so you may wish to consider cycling distance and walking distance.

Equally important is the college's location generally: consider what facilities are nearby, and whether you'd rather be right in the middle of it all or somewhere with more space to yourself.

### Does it have the right facilities?

At this stage it might be useful to consult the Alternative Prospectus provided by students are each university (these can be found on every college website). Students already at Oxbridge are expert at discussing their own colleges' good and bad points. Once you have read them, you can eliminate colleges which don't have a particular facility (such as provision for sports or music). If you're unsure, contact the college directly for clarification. You may think now that all you will do at university is work but you will be grateful that your college has extra facilities such as a decent JCR bar with ping pong tables or playing fields nearby or a fantastic music venue. You may not necessarily want to row for the university but you might have fun rowing for your college, for example. It's worth doing a bit of research into what colleges offer before you make a decision.

## Should I visit the college and check it out?

If you can, you should. Just a wander round the grounds and a look at the current students will probably give you a feeling that a college is or isn't right for you and you are bound to prefer some over others. If you are unable to attend an open day, it is still possible to get a feel for a college by visiting at another time, although you may be restricted in terms of which areas you can explore. You can also ask questions of current students and professors. Each college has its own printed prospectus, which will provide more detailed information than its entry in the university prospectus.

## Should I think about the accommodation?

You'll be spending three or four years at university and the standard of college accommodation varies quite dramatically from college to college. If the size and standard of room matters to you, a bit of research will pay dividends. What's more, some colleges offer accommodation for the whole of your course, whereas at others you may find yourself competing against everyone else in the private rental sector (and 'living out' can prove more costly as you will have to rent a flat or house for the whole of the academic year, not just during term time).

## Should I make a tactical decision?

So you're nearly there. You're close to deciding on your choice of university and your course. Lots of people now try to make a tactical choice based on which colleges are less popular, less centrally located, less well endowed; the theory being that somehow they'll be easier to get into. But don't be fooled. There is no clever way around the system. Don't waste any time worrying about it.

Just because a college is smaller or out of the way (such as Girton at Cambridge) or has fewer applicants per place offered (such as St Hilda's at Oxford), you should not think that this will give you a higher chance of a place. Despite the fact that a few colleges often receive less than one applicant per place offered (check the Oxford admissions website, for example), it does not mean that every direct applicant is offered a place, merely that many of their successful applicants come from the pooling system. Both Oxford and Cambridge put a lot of effort into inter-college 'moderation' to ensure that your chances do not depend on which college you applied to. You might be the only applicant to your chosen college for your chosen course and still not be offered a place. Choose your first preference based on where you think you might be happy, rather than where you think you have the 'best' chance.

> ### Case study: Maddie, Balliol College, Oxford
>
> Choosing a college was one of the few things I remember enjoying about applying to Oxford. I sat by the fire (it really is that cold in Leeds in September!) with a hot chocolate and the college-guide prospectus and read it like a magazine (looking mainly at the pictures!). As I was applying to study physics and philosophy, my college choice was limited to those which offered the subject, but within this group, I indulged in making lots of sweeping generalisations (looks like they work all the time at Merton, all sports people at Teddy Hall, all Thespians at Worchester, etc.) none of which turned out to be true. I then convinced my parents that it was imperative that I booked time off school to visit all the colleges, and spent a lovely couple of days sightseeing with my friend. In the end though, neither the 'alternative prospectuses' nor the college buildings were very decisive. I finally chose Balliol because it had a very good reputation, was high but not top of the Norrington Table, and had a large intake of phys-phil-ers.
>
> Having spent four years at Balliol the thing I liked most about it was the particularly varied student body. The college prides itself on accepting people from all backgrounds and from all over the

world, making for a vibrant and boisterous undergraduate community. I also enjoyed being at a college where several people studied physics and philosophy as it was much less horrible to do tutorial problem sheets all together, than to be stuck struggling through them on your own. The one downside to Balliol was that we did seem to doing a bit more work and be under more pressure than my friends from other colleges (but then again this might have been in my mind!!!). Overall the best thing about studying at Oxford was the people I met and the friends I made. It was brilliant (and exhausting!) to spend four years surrounded by so many inspiring people.

# 6| Experience to support your application

Everything about your Oxbridge application needs to be convincing if you are to present yourself in the best possible light. We have already discussed the importance of being able to show that you have read around your subject and that you have delved far beyond the standard exam texts in your desire to find out more about your subject. But what else can you do that will set your application apart?

Work experience is essential if you think you want to study a vocational subject such as law or medicine, and it is important that you explore how you are going to organise this well in advance. It is naïve to think that you can arrange work experience at short notice; you will need to ask the advice of your parents, friends and school to help you arrange something worthwhile and you must plan ahead. Ideally you will have arranged several bursts of relevant work experience.

It is important to keep your eyes and ears open to relevant events that you could attend in your area, newspaper articles that relate to your subject, blogs, radio programmes and any other sources of information that might give your application an additional dimension. A whole range of companies have in the past offered gap-year programmes; for example, the big four accountancy firms (PricewaterhouseCoopers, KPMG, Deloitte, Accenture), as well as IBM, Bank of England and Rothschild. There is also Year-in-Industry who specialise in a broad range of year-long gap-year placements.

## Gap years

There has been much debate recently about the value of gap years. You will need to decide whether to make an application for deferred entry (this is when you apply whilst doing your A levels, two years in advance of your first term at university) or to apply a year after your school friends do, whilst you are on your year out. When making this decision you should ring your college of choice to discuss their preferences.

### Can I take a gap year and defer my entry?

Some Cambridge and Oxford colleges do not like making offers to deferred entrants, simply because this means they have to commit a place before they have met competing applicants for the following year. In this case, colleges encourage you to wait a year and apply whilst on your gap year. If you ask their advice and make the most of your time out you will find that most colleges are happy for you to have a gap year. In allowing yourself time to mature you may even make a better application and become a more attractive candidate. But you should be aware that if you apply pre-A level and ask for a gap year, you may be swaying your odds of being offered a place against you. For example, at Trinity College Oxford, nine places to read English were available but only two were offered to gap-year students.

Cambridge states that about one in 10 students take a gap year before starting their studies. They acknowledge that a year out can be a very useful time in which to improve skills, earn money, travel and generally gain maturity and self-reliance. They ask that you state on your UCAS application if you wish to defer entry. You'll almost certainly be asked about your plans at interview, so you need to be prepared to talk about what you hope to do and achieve in your gap year.

If you're applying for Mathematics, most colleges have a preference for immediate entry. However, if you're applying for Engineering many colleges generally prefer applicants to take a year out, to gain some industrial experience. You will not be able to defer entry for the Graduate Course in Medicine.

What about Oxford? Some commentators will say that it isn't true that you can't get in if you take a gap year; for instance, Oxford made 6.4% of offers last year to gap-year students, with 6.7% of applicants applying to start post-gap year. This is an insignificant difference, demonstrating that taking a gap year may do your chances of getting an offer no harm. However, if you do opt to take a gap year, it is important that you choose to do something worthwhile, ideally which emphasises your enthusiasm for the subject.

It's important to understand that each college has a different point of view about gap years and you must check the college's website to ensure you know what their opinion is. For example, here's what Merton College says:

> 'Applications for deferred entry are welcomed for all subjects taken by the College, except Physics and the beginners' Russian course. Candidates should be aware that in many subjects, applicants who are offered places for deferred entry will generally be among the strongest of the cohort for their subject. A number of deferred entry applicants may be offered a non-deferred place instead. For more detail on individual subjects' deferred entry policies, please check departmental websites.'

Some tutors in Physics do not encourage deferred entry, largely because lack of practice can affect the mathematical competence achieved at A level or equivalent. They will, however, consider applications in certain special circumstances, e.g. where a candidate sponsored by industry is spending a year in a laboratory.

It is very helpful if all applicants planning a gap year explain briefly what their plans entail on their application form.

# Work experience

### What kind of work experience is best?

Any kind of work experience will be useful. Just getting used to the routine of working in an office, shop, restaurant or factory can come as quite a shock. Getting to work on time, dressing appropriately, getting on with your work colleagues, coping with boredom as well as stress are all valuable lessons in life skills.

Ideally though, you should try to find work experience that relates to the subject you hope to study at university. Experience within the work environment is particularly important if you want to study a vocational subject, for example law or medicine. It is often only in a work situation that one can fully understand the stresses, responsibilities and pleasures that go along with a particular career, and only then can you really commit. Work experience can provide admissions tutors with strong evidence that candidates are committed, determined and have thought through their applications carefully. It can also provide you with a goal that keeps you motivated even through the toughest periods of study.

Apart from having a real idea of where you might be in five years' time, work experience can expose you to ideas related to the subject you are about to study in exciting ways. For example, if you want to study science subjects at Oxford or Cambridge, you might try to get a week during school holidays helping or observing at a laboratory where the scientists are working on something you are particularly interested in. You will be able to sit in on lab meetings and hear for yourself the problems that they face and the solutions they come to. You can also ask them personally for reading suggestions. No one will be as ahead of the game as they are and this will give you some really exciting things to discuss at interview.

If you are really serious about studying and learning, find a way to get more information within the work environment. This will not only give you greater knowledge and confidence, it will also show the admissions tutors that you are really interested.

### How do I organise my work experience?

It's never too early to start planning your work experience and the really ambitious student will aim to organise several sessions.

It will be difficult in the current economic climate to persuade companies to let you join them, but if you are persistent and imaginative you will find openings.

**First, do your research.** Search online to find out about companies and institutions that operate in your field of study. What about think tanks and other, more academic organisations or publishing houses that produce literature for your chosen subject?

**Next, find someone in your chosen organisation to contact.** Never send a letter to a company or organisation without finding an appropriate person to address it to; the more senior, the better. Letters that are sent without a specific recipient usually end up in the accounts department!

**Write a winning introductory letter.** Say exactly what you're looking for in terms of job opportunities, when you want to join and what you feel you can offer their company.

**Attach the perfect CV.** Brief, accurate, with no typing errors or grammatical or spelling mistakes.

**Include a couple of references.** Perhaps one from a teacher at your school and one from another responsible adult who has been impressed by your resourcefulness or past endeavours.

**Email a few days after you've posted your letters.** Quite often, your email will go straight to the relevant person if you type their full name with a stop in the middle and then their company name, e.g. joe.brown@ multinational.com. It is worth a try!

**Follow up.** if you haven't had a response, phone a week later and ask if they received your application. Be very polite. Good luck!

### Case study: Tracy, Chemistry, Jesus College, Oxford

Since coming to study in England my ambition has been to study chemistry at Oxford. I knew that I needed to get some work experience during the summer before I applied so that I would have something unusual to say when I got to the interview, and something meaty to add to my personal statement. I come from Beijing, in China, so before I went home for the summer I contacted my parents and told them I needed some work experience. They spoke to their friends, and, magically, a friend of a friend had a contact with a research lab in my home city. When I went home for the summer I spent two weeks working in that research lab. It was really interesting, as they were developing some new chemicals that could be really helpful in developing drugs to cure terminal illnesses. I asked so many questions, and had the opportunity to help out a bit with their experiments. Mostly I watched, but that didn't matter. The experience really confirmed for me that I wanted to make science – and in particular chemistry – a career. I felt so passionate about it, and I guess the interviewers saw this, because I got a place!

## Events in your area

If you want to study a humanities subject, particularly a subject that is not vocational, keeping up to date with current affairs and events in your area is perhaps even more important than work experience. If you are really passionate about your subject, and dedicated to getting a place at Oxford or Cambridge, you should be constantly on the lookout for local events that are relevant to the subject that you want to study. Local libraries often host talks by renowned authors, the Royal Institute and the Science Museum in London host regular science lectures, the Royal Geographic Society organises regular discussions with eminent geographers and the Royal Academy of Art has an ongoing art history lecture series. In addition, the universities in your area may hold lectures that could interest you. Speak to your teachers for ideas or go online to search for relevant events.

Ideas you might consider include:

- politics: go on a tour of the Houses of Parliament
- law: sit in the public gallery of your local Magistrates' or Crown Court
- history and archaeology: visit the British Museum
- art and history of art: visit every gallery and museum you can get to, including the galleries local to Oxford and Cambridge.

You should also be aware of news stories that relate to developments in your field. Try to get as big a picture as possible about your subject: about how it relates to the rest of the word and why it might be important to know about it. Keep up to date with relevant blogs and think tanks, read the newspapers online and listen to podcasts.

### Case study: Ella, History, Cambridge

When I was writing my personal statement for UCAS and preparing for my interview I spent hours reading articles in the press and visiting museums and historical sites. I was interested in the whole concept of 'history' and how it impacts on us in society and our everyday lives. I wanted to make sure that I had really thought deeply and philosophically about the subject I wanted to study, so that I wouldn't be caught out by strange interview questions, and so I had strong opinions of my own.

I visited quite a lot of museums in London, particularly the British Museum, and this helped to put in perspective just how subjective the telling of history can be. I mean, the British Museum is a collection of artefacts which were brought together when Britain was an empire. The grand building continues to create a picture of the UK as a powerful nation with intellectual superiority and political reach. And although things have changed since it was first open – slavery has been abolished, the colonies are no more – we continue to frame our past in the same way.

In addition to visiting exhibitions and museums I listened to radio broadcasts by historians and thinkers that opened my mind to different concepts, completely separate from anything I had thought about at school. The radio programme In Our Time is a favourite of mine. I also read the papers every day, and cut out any article that I thought was important. I realised that the political slants given in news stories by journalists could be seen in official history, and I came to consider history as a subjective narrative.

I hadn't had any relevant work experience when I was planning my application, so I wanted to do something practical that showed I could think on my feet. I had gone to a talk on 'British Identity' at the Tate Britain and was really excited about the idea that the notion of 'identity' could be something fluid and shaped by many different subjective historical narratives. I wanted to understand how 'history' shapes people's lives today. I wrote a questionnaire and took it first to all my friends and family, and then to neighbours and finally to friendly looking people on the street. I got some really interesting answers.

Having my eyes open and consciously absorbing information from all around me was, I think, the reason I got an offer to start studying history at Cambridge in October 2011.

# 7 | The UCAS application and the personal statement

So finally you are ready to apply. The next stage is arguably the one that causes students the most anxiety. Your UCAS application will need to be submitted by the closing date for all Oxbridge applications of 15 October.

Let's go through the practicalities step by step.

## Step one: Preparing your UCAS application

The online form will be the same as for every other university: through the University and Colleges Admissions Service (UCAS). The UCAS form is a long document that is completed online and sent to all five of your chosen universities. It asks you to include details of your school(s), exam grades, employment experience, your choices of university in order of preference and a personal statement: a 47-line written document that outlines the reasons for your choice of subject.

We will look more closely at what makes a winning personal statement later in this chapter.

You will need to specify a campus code in your 'courses' section. For most universities, this will be 'main site', but for collegiate universities such as Cambridge and Oxford, you need to state the college you wish to apply to from the list, or select 'Open', if you are not concerned about naming a specific college.

## Step two: References

You will need to tell your school or college that you wish to apply to Oxbridge as soon as possible. If they have lots of candidates who have applied before, the staff will be aware of what the colleges are looking for from the academic reference. If your school has little experience of making Oxbridge applications, the universities will probably be aware of this anyway and base their decision more on your personal statement and grades. But it is worth reminding your referees of the early deadline and making sure they'll have your reference ready on time.

You will also need to confirm that your school has submitted the Special Access Scheme form to Cambridge, if you are eligible to apply through this scheme.

## Step three: External tests

You must check whether the universities require you to sit any special tests such as the BMAT or LNAT. See Chapter 8 for more details.

## Step four: Supplementary questionnaires

### Cambridge

Once you've submitted your UCAS form, you will receive an acknowledgement almost immediately from Cambridge by email, along with their Supplementary Application Questionnaire (SAQ), which will require completion by the following week.

The SAQ is filled out online, costs nothing to send and gives Cambridge more information about you and your application. If you do not have access to email you can contact the Cambridge Admissions Office for a paper version.

The initial email will give you all the information you need in order to complete the form correctly, as well as a deadline (usually the end of October).

The SAQ includes the following eight sections.

1. **Photograph.** You will need a passport-sized colour photograph of yourself, preferably in digital format, which can then be uploaded onto the form.
2. **Application type.** This section asks questions about your application, such as whether you have applied for an organ scholarship, if you are taking a gap year or whether you are going through the Special Access Scheme.
3. **Personal details.** This covers information about you and your own situation, such as where you live, what your first name is, etc.
4. **Course details.** Here you need to declare your preferred course options (if applicable); for example, if you are applying to read modern and medieval languages, you state which languages you wish to study in this section.
5. **Education.** In this section, you will need to give information about your school(s), such as class sizes and descriptions of any extra help you may have received towards your application.
6. **Qualifications.** In this section, you need to give details of your AS and/or A level modules, or their equivalents, and your marks.
7. **Additional information.** This is where you can add an additional personal statement. You will also need to discuss your career plans

and give some proof of your interest in your chosen subject (for example, details of your work experience).

8. **Submit.**

The additional personal statement is the perfect opportunity for you to explain to the admissions tutor how excited you are about the course and perhaps the college to which you are applying. Do take advantage of this extra space to make an impression.

Remember, however, not to duplicate anything you have said on the UCAS form. While your UCAS personal statement will be seen by every institution you apply to, the SAQ is for the admissions tutors at Cambridge only. This means that you can discuss particular elements of the course content or programme at Cambridge without putting any other university off. Make the most of this and explain why their course and teaching staff are perfect for you, and why you will fit in particularly well there.

Remember also that by mentioning your areas of special academic interest, you will encourage predictable questions at interview, making it easier to prepare thoroughly.

## Oxford

Your chosen college at Oxford will usually be fairly swift in confirming that they have received your application and they will write requesting any further information they require. If you have made an open application, the college to which you have been allocated will respond.

Oxford no longer requires any additional forms, apart from the following three exceptions:

1. candidates for choral or organ awards
2. candidates wishing to be interviewed overseas
3. graduate applicants for the Accelerated Medical Course.

## Step five: Submitting written work

Another way admissions tutors decide whether or not to interview you – if you are applying for an essay-based subject – is by looking at a sample of your written work. This is something that you need to consider once you have submitted your application form(s). By looking at one of your essays, the admissions tutors will be able to assess your ability to research, organise information, form opinions and construct a coherent and cogent argument in writing. These are essential skills to have when studying an essay subject at Oxbridge, and the admissions tutors need to see that you have these skills, and the potential to improve.

Normally the essay that you send will have been written as part of your A level course. Make sure that you send a particularly good example of your work; ask your teachers to suggest changes and then to re-mark the essay when you have improved it as much as possible.

Do not, however, submit anything that could not have been written by you. Plagiarism will be very obvious to admissions tutors and could potentially get you into some tricky situations at interview since submitted written work is often discussed at interview.

> 'The submitted essay is often used as the starting point for discussion in the interview. The essay can show us whether the candidate has the ability to argue and has academic confidence.'
>
> Admissions Tutor, Cambridge

At Cambridge each college has a different policy on written work, but you are more likely to be asked to send in work if you are applying to read an arts or social sciences subject. The college will contact you directly if they require work from you.

The Oxford prospectus gives clear instructions about what you need to send and when. Remember to inform your teachers in advance that you will need to send marked work.

If you have applied to Oxford, you will need to submit marked work for the following subjects:

1. archaeology and anthropology
2. classical archaeology and ancient history
3. classics
4. classics and English
5. classics and modern languages
6. classics and oriental studies
7. economics and management
8. English and modern languages
9. English language and literature
10. European and Middle Eastern languages
11. fine art (portfolio submission)
12. geography
13. history
14. history (ancient and modern)
15. history and economics
16. history and English
17. history and modern languages
18. history and politics
19. modern languages
20. modern languages and linguistics
21. music

22. Oriental studies
23. philosophy and modern languages
24. philosophy and theology
25. theology
26. theology and oriental studies

### Step Six: Await the call for interview!

See Chapter 9 for more advice on interviews.

## How to write your personal statement

This part of the application process can be tortuous if you allow yourself to overcomplicate matters. The quest for the 'perfect PS' is like searching for the Holy Grail. There's no such thing, or if there is, you will have died of exhaustion before you find it.

You might want to remind yourself before you start of what admission tutors are looking for.

> 'We are assessing academic potential and aptitude for studying the chosen subject at degree level. We hope to spot an applicant's future potential through interview questions and admissions tests and to differentiate between applicants with the same predicted A level grades. We value intellectual flexibility, clarity of thought, analytical skills and the ability to argue logically. It's also important that we see evidence of enthusiasm for and commitment to the chosen course. This is usually demonstrated by lots of reading around a subject, work experience and relevant hobbies, which can all demonstrate an applicant's commitment to their chosen course. We also try to assess the student's level of motivation and self-discipline. The Cambridge system of teaching and learning requires students to be extremely self-disciplined and hard-working. If a candidate has successfully balanced school or college work with other commitments (family, work, hobbies) that is usually a good indicator that they will cope well at university.'
> Sidney Sussex College Cambridge's Admissions Department

Think of things from the admission tutor's point of view. What constitutes a great personal statement as far as they're concerned? Most candidates will present themselves with excellent grades, predicted or actual, and glowing references from their teachers. They may also have taken specific admission tests or submitted written work. The personal statement is one more element that the staff can use to judge whether or not a candidate will be suitable for their courses. Most Admission Tutors are keen to stress that all candidates' applications are viewed 'in the round'. Be assured they are not expecting your personal statement to be a literary masterpiece or a work of stunning originality. They want to hear about you, in particular:

- what interests you about your chosen subject (and why)
- why you want to study the subject(s) you've applied for
- what you have learnt or done outside your college or school syllabus
- which activities you've participated in that have added to your knowledge of your subject
- what you do apart from studying and why is this important to you
- what you hope to do after you've finished university, if you currently have an idea.

## How to get started - some dos and dont's

**Do** take time to submit something that is well written; i.e. the grammar and spelling should be correct, and you should write in sentences rather than a list. Ask your teacher or someone you trust to read it through carefully for mistakes.

**Do** go into detail. It's better to write in detail about a few topics than try to cite lots of interesting topics in a cursory way. Use examples to demonstrate your understanding of your subject so far and your desire to explore your subject further.

**Do** justify everything that you put down on paper. 'I found going to lectures at the LSE fascinating' only begs the question 'Why?'

**Don't** be tempted to just list the books that you have read; explain how reading them enriched your learning or excited you and made you want to read around your subject. Similarly, please don't tell them that you've read the obvious choices; when the 20th Economics applicant says that they've enjoyed *Freakonomics* even the most well-disposed tutor will marvel at a student's lack of ingenuity.

**Don't** use long, convoluted sentences that are hard to follow; the admissions tutor may lose concentration before he or she reaches the end of the paragraph.

**Don't** lie; you will get found out. If you are lucky enough to be called for interview you will be asked about your personal statement and although you may not remember that you said that you read and enjoyed Nietzsche's *Twilight of the Idols*, the tutor interviewing you will. Be warned!

**Don't** be tempted to spend too much time listing your achievements outside of school. No more than a third of your personal statement should be devoted to non-academic matters.

Many schools who are very successful at getting their students into Oxbridge adopt a fairly formulaic approach to writing personal statements. This is certainly one way of making your life a little easier and it might help you on your first draft. But remember, the key to writing your personal statement is that it should be **personal**; if you allow lots of people to read yours, you will receive lots of different opinions on its strengths and weaknesses. This can be confusing, to say the least. In the end, the best advice is to decide what you want to say and say it with conviction, in your own words, not those of your parents, teachers or other advisers.

## A model Oxbridge personal statement

There are no hard and fast rules about how to structure your personal statement. Below, however, is an example of how a well-organised statement might be written with a synopsis, paragraph by paragraph. Each synopsis is an example of a paragraph written by a candidate who did get a place at Oxford to study history and ancient history. Read the example carefully, but do not be tempted to copy it.

The first paragraph should explain what sparked your interest in your chosen subject and why you wish to study it at university.

My passion for history and ancient history began, perhaps unusually, in the genre of historical novels, and the more general histories of those such as Norwich and Goldsworthy. These originally caught my imagination with their sweeping narratives of the Roman military world, and the world of late antiquity. This swiftly sparked an interest in more specific and more scholarly works, such as Syme's, 'The Roman Revolution', which made me think differently about my assumptions of the power of individuals; in this case Augustus' role as the product of a talented new ruling class, rather than as a lone genius, as well as Scullard's, 'From the Gracchi to Nero', on the challenges which Rome faced internally, as she externally became a superpower, and the necessary changes which the fall of the republic would later bring about.

In paragraph two you could discuss your particular interests in relation to your university subject choice. This is your chance to write about specific ideas you have developed as a result of reading beyond your A level syllabus. Paragraphs one and two should take up about two-thirds of the entire statement.

What perhaps fascinates me the most is the way in which history, particularly in the distant past, is perceived by the succeeding generations of scholars, either through a difference of opinion in scholarly debate, or as a natural result of their environment. For example, Gibbon's demonisation of the Byzantine Empire, despite hardly being based in historical fact, is easy to understand in the context of the founding of the European world empires and The Enlightenment. Another example of this is the illusion of the founding of nations during the dark ages, and the tendency of historians to link the kingdoms of the dark ages with the modern states they were to form later on. Christopher Wickham's discussion of this phenomenon, in his 'The Inheritance of Rome' interested me immensely, as it made me question the blind belief which I had shown before when reading the narrative history of this period. Perhaps in a less orthodox way, I was also heavily influenced by Terry Jones' protestations at the misinterpretation of Celtic culture in his study, 'Barbarians'. Though clearly it is difficult to make assertions about an empire without trusting your sources to some degree, it is nevertheless hugely interesting to read history from a contrary viewpoint.

The third paragraph can start to incorporate your personal experiences and how these have shaped your academic interests and choice of university subject.

Another stimulating part of studying both history and ancient history is the way in which one can see how different cultures have left their mark on a particular place. A good example of this, particularly in an ancient context, is in Tunisia, where the Phoenicians, the Carthaginians, the Romans, the Vandals, the Byzantines and the Arabs have all left their mark in the numerous sites, which are fascinating both in the context of ancient and modern history. To follow this up, therefore, independently, I have done a week-long trip, in which I did a route involving retracing Cato's last march, as well as looking at the ruins of Jugurtha's capital at Beja, which has since seen many conquerors, the Byzantine fortress at Kelibia, the remarkable Arabic city of Kairouan, and the Roman ruins at Dougga. One piece of extended work which I have done this summer, has been on the Jugurthine war, and the other was on Justinian's capture of Africa from the Vandals. I have also used my trip to supplement my research, as well as to develop much further my knowledge of post-Almohad Tunisian history.

The fourth paragraph can include a brief summary of your extra-curricular activities. Remember, the admissions tutor will have to live with you for three years if you get in to his or her college. You need to come across as a responsible, interesting person who will be an asset to the college.

Outside of the academic sphere, my main passion is music. I play the double bass to grade seven standard, and have recently started the jazz double bass, as well as enjoying collecting vinyl records. I have also attended many Model United Nations meetings, which I have enjoyed and have excelled in, particularly those set in historical situations. I am also interested in journalism, in which I have done work experience, and I would hope to contribute to magazines at University. My reading, though mostly focused on history, also encompasses literature, and I am particularly interested in the great American novel, having been moved by the work of Fitzgerald, Hemingway and Capote, as well as the works of Leo Tolstoy, Maxim Gorky, and Fyodor Dostoyevsky.

## The UCAS application

1. Go to www.ucas.com/students/apply to register in September. In order to do this you will need an email address. If you haven't got one go to www.yahoo.com or www.hotmail.com and get a free one. When you register on the UCAS website, you will be sent an application number, user name and password, which you will need every time you log on to UCAS.

2. The entire application is done online and although it may seem complex and time-consuming, you can complete it in stages and come back to it. There are 'help' sections all the way through the form in case you get stuck.

3. Fill in the 'Personal details' section, which includes your name, address and date of birth.

4. Fill in the 'Student support' section, which is where you have to select your fee code. If you are a British national your local authority will be your fee payer.

5. Next is an 'Additional information' section in which you can list the activities you have done in preparation for further education. These activities specifically refer to attending summer schools in preparation for university run by either the universities themselves or trusts such as the Sutton Trust. See www.suttontrust.com/home or contact UCAS for more information (www.ucas.com/about_us/contact_us).

6. The fifth section is where you enter your 'University choices'. You can apply to either Oxford or Cambridge. Choose the correct university code from the drop-down menu (CAM C05 for Cambridge and OXF 033 for Oxford). You also need to write what UCAS calls the 'campus code', which is the college code. A drop-down list will appear again. You will also need to choose the subject and select which year of entry you are applying for.

7. The next section asks you for details of your education. You need to write down every GCSE and A level (or equivalent qualification) you have taken and what grade you got under the heading of the school in which you took them. If you are applying post-A level you need to write down all of your module grades.

8. The next section is 'Employment'. This does not ask you about work experience, but about paid employment. It is worth writing down even the most insignificant jobs you have done – washing dishes at the local restaurant, for example – since admissions tutors will value the commitment and maturity you will have shown when holding down a job.

9. Next is the 'Personal statement'. This is your chance to show the admissions tutors how you write and how informed you are about your subject. You should write this in a Word document, spell check it and read it through carefully and when it is ready, copy and paste it into the UCAS form.

10. Finally, send the application in the first week of October to be completed by your teachers. In order to do this, you have to pay £22 (or £11 if you are applying to just one university) to UCAS to process your information. This must be paid by credit card (your school may have a policy of paying this for you so you need to check before you part with any money). Your teacher will then be able to open it on the teachers' part of the UCAS site. They will read it to check everything is correct and will then write their reference and predicted grades. Your teacher may need some time to write the reference, so do make sure you have your part done well in advance.

11. Your teachers then need to send your UCAS application to Oxford and Cambridge by 15 October. This will arrive at the universities immediately.

# 8 | Succeeding in written tests

Over the past few years, more and more students are achieving As and A*s at A level. As it has become harder to identify academically outstanding students through their A level results, both Oxford and Cambridge now rely on additional testing systems when selecting candidates for interview. The following chapter aims to give an account of the various written tests students face prior to or during their interviews, including the deadlines for registering for the exams; when and where the tests are sat; details about the structure of the tests, including knowledge requirements; sample questions; and useful links for more information and practice.

These tests include the BMAT for medicine and the LNAT for law at Oxford, two externally administered tests. The HAT is taken for history at Oxford and there are various similar but internal exams set by Cambridge colleges. STEP papers (Sixth Term Examination Papers) have been reintroduced for maths at Cambridge as well as the TSA (Thinking Skills Assessment) for various other Oxford and Cambridge subjects. These exams aim to highlight the natural intelligence and academic potential of the candidate and in doing so, widen access. Since it is often difficult to revise for the Oxbridge written tests, students have to rely on their innate intellectual ability to complete them. In theory, students whose schools have provided less preparation should not be disadvantaged.

The style of testing also differs from what many school leavers will be used to. Whereas A levels often test factual recall, the Oxbridge written exams look for analytical and critical capabilities. It should be noted, therefore, that these tests are likely to be much harder than anything you will have experienced at school. This is taken into consideration, and admissions tutors do not expect students to achieve 100%.

Oxford and Cambridge take different approaches to additional written tests in some subjects. Oxford exams are standardised: for example, all students applying for history across the whole university will take exactly the same test (the HAT). In contrast, Cambridge tests vary from college to college.

Testing happens at various stages during the application process. Some tests are sat in early November at your school. The results of these tests can then play a part in determining whether you are called to interview. Some tests – including the majority of those for Cambridge – take place when you go up for interview in early December. The results are then used, alongside your interview performance, your personal statement, your school references and your exam grades to decide whether you should be made a conditional offer.

**Table 2:** Entrance exam deadlines

| Exam | Exam entries start date | Exam entries standard deadline | Cost | Exam date | Results released |
|---|---|---|---|---|---|
| TSA Oxford | 1 Sep 2011 | 14 Oct 2011 4pm | No cost | Wed 7 Nov 2012 | 14 Jan 2013 |
| ELAT | 1 Sep 2012 | 15 Oct 2012 5pm | No cost | Wed 7 Nov 2012 | 14 Jan 2013 |
| BMAT | 1 Sep 2012 | 15 Oct 2012 | Standard £42.50 Late £72.50 | Wed 7 Nov 2012 | 21 Nov 2012 |
| HAT | 1 Sep 2012 | 15 October 2012 5pm | No cost | Wed 7 Nov 2012 | T.B.C |
| PAT | 1 Sep 2012 | 15 Oct 2012 5pm | No cost | Wed 7 Nov 2012 | T.B.C |
| TSA Cambridge | Cambridge will arrange the test sitting when candidate goes for interview. | | | | |
| UKCAT | Students need to register themselves for these exams through the website www.ukcat.ac.uk | | | | |
| LNAT | Students need to register themselves for these exams through the website www.lnat.ac.uk | | | | |
| STEP | Dates not yet released for 12/13 entry but entries aren't normally made until March. | | | | |

Don't let taking these tests put you off applying. If you are serious about wanting a place at a top university, you should be able to do well without masses of additional tuition or extra work. It is very important, however, to go online and get full details of what the tests entail and to do some practice papers if they are offered.

## Oxford admission tests

### 1 October 2012
Standard deadline for registering for the BioMedical Admissions Test (BMAT)

**15 October 2012**
Final deadline for registering for the BioMedical Admissions Test (BMAT), the English Literature Admissions Test (ELAT), the History Aptitude Test (HAT), the Physics Aptitude Test (PAT) and the Thinking Skills Assessment (TSA)

**15 October 2012**
Closing date for all UCAS applications
Closing date for receipt of application forms for the accelerated medical course

**1 September–20 October 2012**
Law National Admissions Test (LNAT)

**7 November 2012**
BioMedical Admissions Test (BMAT)
English Literature Admissions Test (ELAT)
History Aptitude Test (HAT)
Physics Aptitude Test (PAT)
Aptitude Test for Mathematics and Computer Science
Thinking Skills Assessment (TSA)
Tests for all Modern Languages courses
Tests for all Classics courses

# Cambridge admission tests

## Thinking Skills Assessment Test (TSA)

You may be asked to take the Cambridge Thinking Skills Assessment test, either online or on paper, when you come for interview. This test assesses critical thinking and problem-solving skills and is used by a number of colleges for the following courses:

- Chemical Engineering
- Computer Science
- Economics
- Engineering
- Land Economy
- Natural Sciences
- Politics, Psychology and Sociology.

There's no need to register in advance for the TSA (Cambridge) and there's no charge associated with the test. The college dealing with your application will contact you about the arrangements if they're using it.

### Biomedical Assessment Test (BMAT)

All applicants for medicine and veterinary medicine are required to take this test after making their application and before interview. The test is used to assess scientific aptitude and focuses on scientific abilities relevant to the study of medicine and veterinary medicine.

The BMAT is also used by some other universities.

Applicants are responsible for ensuring they enter for the BMAT by 1 October 2012. The BMAT test will be on 7 November 2012.

There is an entry fee for this test and details and available on the BMAT website. UK applicants in receipt of certain financial support may apply for their BMAT fees to be reimbursed. Please contact the BMAT Support Team for more information.

### Cambridge Law Test

Most colleges require applicants for Law to take the Cambridge Law Test, which is designed to provide an assessment of your potential for the Cambridge law course. It's used as an additional piece of information alongside your school/college examination results, the other information provided in your application, and your performance at interview when making admissions decisions.

Applicants take the test when they're in Cambridge for interview and are required to answer one question in one hour. (Applicants who are interviewed overseas sit a slightly different version of the test, see the Faculty of Law website for details). No prior knowledge of the law is required or expected. You don't need to register in advance – your college will contact you about the arrangements – and there's no charge associated with taking the Cambridge Law Test.

## Specimen papers for Oxbridge tests

### BMAT

*Section 1 (2010 paper)*

62 trillion spam emails are sent every year, amounting to emissions of more than 17 million tons of carbon dioxide, one of the main contributors to global warming. More effective spam filtering could reduce the amount by 75%, which would be the equivalent of taking 2.3 million cars off the road. This would not deal with the extra energy being used to send out the messages in the first place, however. A better strategy would be to fight spam at the source. When one global web hosting firm was taken offline after it was found to have ties to spammers, global spam volume fell briefly by 70%.

Which one of the following is a conclusion that could be drawn from the above passage?

A   It is always better to fight problems at the source.
B   Reducing spam is a higher priority than easing congestion on the roads.
C   Action to deal with global warming should include tackling spam as one of the strategies.
D   Spam filtering systems should be improved as much as possible.
E   Action to stop spam will never have long lasting effects.

During the trial of a 10 year old accused of frequent violent crimes, privacy laws meant that he could only be referred to in the media as 'Child B'. One newspaper, however, continually referred to the boy as the 'Devil Child'. Despite many media sources reporting the difficult and violent upbringing the boy himself had had, calling for understanding and leniency, many letters sent to newspapers and comments posted on internet forums showed strong public anger and calls for the harshest possible sentence. Almost all of those calling for tough measures used the term 'Devil Child'. This shows that the name alone had influenced public opinion and prevented members of the public having sympathy for the child.

Which one of the following statements, if true, would strengthen the argument above?

1.   The newspaper that used the term 'Devil Child' reported the case and the child's upbringing accurately.
2.   The editors of the newspaper that used the term 'Devil Child' also called for the harshest possible punishment.
3.   The newspaper that used the term 'Devil Child' had also continually referred to his victims as 'innocent' and 'defenceless'.

A   1 only
B   2 only
C   3 only
D   1 and 2
E   1 and 3
F   2 and 3

### Section 2 (2010 paper)

I have two containers with different capacities. Initially, the larger one is full of water and the smaller one is empty. I pour water from the larger container into the smaller container until they contain the same volume of water. The volume of water in the large container is now $p$ times its capacity and the volume of water in the small container is $q$ times its capacity.

Which one of the following statements about p and q must be true?

A   p + q = 1 (but p and q are not necessarily both 0.5)
B   p = 0.5 and q = 0.5
C   p = 0.5 and q > 0.5
D   p > 0.5 and q = 0.5
E   p > 0.5 and q > 0.5

A car of mass 800kg moves up an incline of 1 in 20 (1 in 20 means for every 20m along the road the car gains 1m in height) at a constant speed of 20m/s. The frictional force opposing motion is 500N.

How much work has been done by the engine after the car has moved 50m?

A   20kJ
B   25kJ
C   27kJ
D   45kJ
E   65kJ
F   160kJ

## Section 3 (2010 paper)

'Anyone who has a serious ambition to be a president or prime minister is the wrong kind of person for the job.'

What is the reasoning behind this statement? Argue to the contrary that without serious ambition to be a leader a person would not be suited to the job. To what extent is ambition required to succeed as a political leader?

'A pet belongs to its owner – it is their property. Thus, if a client asks for their healthy cat to be painlessly euthanised, a veterinary clinician should always agree to this request.'

Explain the reasoning behind the statement. Argue to the contrary that a veterinary clinician should never agree to such a request. To what extent should pet owners influence clinicians' decisions?

From the specimen papers available on the Cambridge Assessment website (www.admissionstests.cambridgeassessment.org.uk). Reprinted by permission of the University of Cambridge Local Examinations Syndicate.

## ELAT (English Literature Apitude Test) (2010 paper)

The following poems and extracts from longer texts offer different perspectives on language and the way people speak. They are arranged in reverse chronological order by date of composition or publication. Read all the material carefully, and then complete the task below.

(a)  From *Moon Tiger*, a novel by Penelope Lively 1987
(b)  From 'Fred and Madge', a play by Joe Orton 1959
(c)  'Their Lonely Betters', a poem by W.H. Auden 1950
(d)  From *Adam Bede*, a novel by George Eliot 1858
(e)  From 'Resolution and Independence', a poem by William Wordsworth 1802
(f)  From *Oroonoko*, a novel by Aphra Behn 1688

Select two or three of the passages (a) to (f) and compare and contrast them in any ways that seem interesting to you, paying particular attention to distinctive features of structure, language and style. In your introduction, indicate briefly what you intend to explore or illustrate through close reading of your chosen passages.

This task is designed to assess your responsiveness to unfamiliar literary material and your skills in close reading. Marks are not awarded for references to other texts or authors you have studied.

From the specimen papers available on the Cambridge Assessment website (www.admissionstests.cambridgeassessment.org.uk). Reprinted by permission of the University of Cambridge Local Examinations Syndicate.

## HAT (History Aptitude Test) (2007 paper)

This is an adapted extract from a book about Renaissance Europe. Please read through the extract carefully and think about what it is trying to say. You do not need to know anything about the topic or the period to answer the questions below.

What all governments had in common was a striving to extend effective control over their subjects and to link the most common contemporary meaning of the word 'state' – the power structure, that is, represented by a ruler and his ministers and chief officials – to the significance of what was then a less familiar usage: the state as a geographical catchment area of individuals owing a common obedience to central government. Whatever the terminology employed, the aim was the same: to make a ruler potent and unchallenged within his whole kingdom, to extend effective administration across it, to stimulate shared responses within the commonwealth of compatriots. The aim was hampered by earlier and stubbornly held assumptions about the government's function: to preserve, and if judged appropriate extend, territory that had been won in the past; to protect legally defined privileges while striving to ensure that all men had access to 'good justice'; to tax sparingly, for the common good and with advice; to foster the rights and influence of 'true religion'. These were conservative values. When rulers, whether a king of France or a doge of Venice, swore to observe them at their coronation or election, they vowed in effect to stop the historical process in its tracks.

Yet in all cases, governments were forced to alter the status quo by the need to raise more money. As the tempo of international relations quickened from the later fifteenth century, the costs of diplomacy, from ambassadors to spies, rose to match their pace. The size of armies grew: from 12–30,000 before 1500, to 85,000 in the 1570s, to 100,000 and more by the 1620s. Better cannon meant that fortresses and town walls had to be rebuilt or strengthened. And war could throw up massive extras: to redeem the sons Francis I of France had left in Spain after his capture at the battle of Pavia in 1525 cost the equivalent of 3.6 tons of solid gold. As all governments were forced throughout the sixteenth century to spend more on war or defence or both, revenues had to rise: in France, for example, from 3.5 million livres in 1497 to 15 million in 1596, in Castile from 850,000 ducats in 1504 to 13 million in 1598. Overall in the course of the century state revenues rose by a factor of five. This was mainly due to the necessities of war, partly to voluntary expenditure on buildings and on lavish courts to inflate the ruler's image. It was also due to larger government payrolls. However ingenious governments were at postponing taxes by raising bridging loans from financiers, repayments, like normal expenditure, had to be met from internal revenues. And this involved extending the reach of administrative fingers into pockets previously guarded from them.

To do this, and to ensure the law and order that made administration effective, more officials had to be maintained. At the lowest level the numbers of copyists and file-clerks and book-keepers employed by earlier governments became inflated. New tasks, notably Spain's acquisition of territories in America and Italy, involved the creation of new governmental committees, but other governments, too, enlarged the departments which had dealt with different aspects of business: finance, foreign affairs, legal issues. Above this proletariat of inky toilers there was a thickening stratum of supervisors who not only co-ordinated the work of their departments but offered advice on knotty or debatable issues. It is at this level of responsibility that their prominence in contemporary records allows them to be counted: between three and four times the number shortly after 1600 than around 1500. In absolute terms this is unimpressive. In mid-sixteenth century France, for instance, with a population of about 18 million, there were no more than three thousand or so. And there were never enough of them, whether operating at the heart of government or in the provinces, to pump obedience along the venous system that connected a capital with a country as a whole to the extent which new legislation called for.

(a) What are the principal points made by the author in the first paragraph? Use your own words and do not write more than 15 lines. (10 marks)

(b) Why, in the author's view, did the institutions of government grow in the period under discussion? Write an answer of about one side in length. (20 marks)

(c) In an essay of two or three sides, identify and discuss the most important factors that changed the relationship between rulers and ruled in a period with which you are familiar. (40 marks)

## Oxford TSA (Thinking Skills Assessment)

### Section 1 (2010 paper)

Splashford Swimming Pool charges £2 per session for adults and £1 for children.

Also available is a Family Swimcard. At a cost of £50, the Family Swimcard allows unlimited use of the pool for one year for 2 adults and up to 3 children. For larger families, every additional child must pay half the children's rate each time.

Mr and Mrs Teal and their 4 children are keen swimmers. They used their Swimcard when the family went swimming 40 times last year.

How much did the Swimcard save the Teal family last year?

A   £50
B   £190
C   £230
D   £250
E   £270

The United States attempts to reduce the supply of illegal drugs by intercepting shipments and eradicating illegal crops. Despite these efforts, illegal drugs are still readily available, because growers, for example those in Colombia, move to different areas and plant smaller plots that are harder to find. So more effort should be made to reduce demand. This does not simply mean reducing the total number of people using illegal drugs. Because the important task is to cut consumption by heavy users, drug-dependent criminals in the country's jails should be treated for their addiction. In this way drug-related social problems can be reduced.

Which one of the following, if true, most strengthens the above argument?

A   The price of drugs has not fallen despite efforts to reduce their supply.
B   Statistics show that many crops of illegal drugs in Colombia have been eradicated.
C   Most of the drug users in US jails do not want treatment for their drug addiction.
D   Heavy drug users are responsible for committing most of the drug-related crime.

E   The majority of the US public are in favour of rehabilitating prisoners who are drug users.

## Section 2 (2010 paper)

'Printing and the telephone were truly revolutionary inventions. All the internet brings is a difference in scale.' Is that true?

If two reasonable people claim the same fact as evidence for opposing conclusions, does it follow that it can't actually be evidence for either?

## Cambridge TSA (specimen paper)

School examination results in England this year reinforce the trend in improving pass rates. There is, however, no other evidence of improvements in school leavers' abilities – such as the data coming from employers or universities. One can reasonably conclude, therefore, that teachers are simply succeeding in coaching their pupils better for examinations than in previous years.

Which one of the following is an underlying assumption of the above argument?

A   School examination results are a reliable indicator of pupils' abilities.
B   The level of difficulty of examinations has not been falling.
C   Employers' expectations of school leavers are unrealistic.
D   Teachers in previous years did not attempt to coach pupils for examinations.
E   Abilities of school pupils vary from year to year.

Ever since Uranus was discovered in 1781, astronomers have thought there might be more planets to be discovered in the Solar System. Because of small deviations in the orbits of Uranus and Neptune – deviations which would occur if another planet existed – some astronomers think there must be an undiscovered planet – Planet X. But the search for Planet X is futile, because these deviations would occur if the orbits had been wrongly predicted. Since Uranus and Neptune take many decades to circle the sun, astronomers must rely on old data in order to calculate their orbits. If this data is inaccurate, the calculated orbits are wrong. If the calculated orbits are wrong, Uranus and Neptune will deviate from them even if there is no Planet X.

Which of the following is the best statement of the flaw in the argument above?

A   From the fact that the old data is inaccurate, it cannot be inferred that the calculated orbits are wrong.
B   From the fact that the data about the orbits is old it cannot be inferred that it is inaccurate.

C   From the fact that deviations occur which would occur if Planet X existed, it cannot be inferred that Planet X exists.
D   From the fact that the calculated orbits are wrong, it cannot be inferred that Uranus and Neptune will deviate from them.
E   From the fact that Planet X has not been discovered, it cannot be inferred that the search for it is futile.

The roller coaster at Blue Top Towers Park runs continuously from 10.00am to 6.00pm during the week and from 9.00am to 7.00pm at weekends.

Each ride lasts for 3 minutes.

It can take up to 5 minutes to unload and reload between rides at busy periods, but even when the park is quiet there is a 2 minute gap between the end of one ride and the beginning of the next.

What is the maximum number of rides there can be in one day?

A   60
B   75
C   96
D   120
E   200

From the specimen papers available on the Cambridge Assessment website (www.admissionstests.cambridgeassessment.org.uk). Reprinted by permission of the University of Cambridge Local Examinations Syndicate.

## LNAT

### Section A

Google is 'white bread for the mind', and the internet is producing a generation of students who survive on a diet of unreliable information, a professor of media studies will claim this week.

In her inaugural lecture at the University of Brighton, Tara Brabazon will urge teachers at all levels of the education system to equip students with the skills they need to interpret and sift through information gleaned from the internet. She believes that easy access to information has dulled students' sense of curiosity and is stifling debate. She claims that many undergraduates arrive at university unable to discriminate between anecdotal and unsubstantiated material posted on the internet and peer-reviewed scholarly research. 'I call this type of education "the University of Google". Google offers easy answers to difficult questions. But students do not know how to tell if they come from serious, refereed work or are merely composed of shallow ideas, superficial surfing and fleeting commitments. Google is white bread for the mind – it is filling but it does not necessarily offer nutritional content,' she said.

Professor Brabazon's concerns echo the author Andrew Keen's criticisms of online amateurism. In his book *The Cult of the Amateur*, Keen says, 'Today's media is shattering the world into a billion personalised truths, each seeming equally valid.'

Professor Brabazon said: 'I've taught all through the digitisation of education. We can no longer assume that students arrive at university knowing what to read and knowing what standards are required of the material that they do read'. 'Students live in an age of information, but what they lack is correct information. They turn to Wikipedia. Why wouldn't they? It's there,' she said.

With libraries in decline, media platforms such as Google made perfect sense. According to Professor Brabazon, the trick was to learn to use them properly. 'We need to teach our students the interpretative skills first before we teach them the technological skills. Students must be trained to be dynamic and critical thinkers rather than drifting to the first site returned through Google,' she said. Her own students are banned from using Wikipedia or Google in their first year of study, but instead are provided with 200 extracts from peer-reviewed printed texts at the beginning of the year, supplemented by printed extracts from eight or nine texts for individual pieces of work. There have been concerns about students plagiarising from the internet and the growth of a new online 'coursework industry', in which websites produce tailor-made essays, some selling for up to £1,000 each.

Wikipedia, containing millions of articles, contributed by users, was founded in 2001. It has been criticised for being riddled with inaccuracies.

Google is the dominant search engine on the internet, it uses a formula designed to place the most relevant content at the top of its listings. But a multimillion-pound industry has grown up concerned with manipulating Google rankings through a process called 'search engine optimisation'.

1. The main criticism in the passage of the use by students of the internet is:
   (a) the material is unsubstantiated
   (b) it means that students use material indiscriminately
   (c) the information is incorrect
   (d) it leads to online amateurism
   (e) it leads to plagiarism

2. What is suggested by the last paragraph?
   (a) There is too much information on Google.
   (b) Students can't distinguish between good and bad content.
   (c) Google has too much power.
   (d) The material isn't always accurate.
   (e) The rankings may not be reliable.

3.  Which of the following is intended to convey approval?
    (a)  'anecdotal'
    (b)  'peer-reviewed'
    (c)  'filling'
    (d)  'equally valid'
    (e)  'tailor-made'

4.  Which of the following comes closest to the meaning of Andrew Keen's criticism?
    (a)  Online information is amateurish.
    (b)  Online information is too easily available.
    (c)  There is too much online information.
    (d)  Online information lacks authority.
    (e)  Students don't know how to use online information effectively.

### Section B: Essay (specimen test)

1.  In what circumstances should abortion be permitted and why?
2.  Would you agree that travel and tourism exploit poorer nations and benefit only the richer ones?
3.  The Olympic Games, today, are less a test of personal athleticism and more a measure of national investment and authority. Do you agree?
4.  Wearing a burkha in Western countries is just as offensive as wearing a bikini in Arab countries. Do you agree?
5.  'Women now have the chance to achieve anything they want.' How do you respond to this statement?

The best way to prepare for these tests is to take advantage of the practice papers provided. You will feel much more comfortable entering your test if you have familiarised yourself with the format and style of question you will be facing.

Sample tests can be found online:
www.admissionstests.cambridgeassessment.org.uk/adt

Sample LNAT tests can be found at:
www.lnat.ac.uk

You could also refer to: *Practise & Pass Professional: LNAT* (Trotman, 2011)

# 9 | Surviving the interview

About four to eight weeks after you have submitted your application, a letter will drop through your door. At this stage you will find out whether you have been called for interview.

If you haven't, don't despair. There's always next year or another university. It's really not the end of the world. If you have been called for interview – congratulations! Now make the most of the opportunity presented to you and do your preparation to make the experience a positive one.

## Prepare properly: The practicalities

If you live a long distance from the universities or have an exam to take, the college may ask you to stay over the night before the interview. Being in college for a night or even a few days will give you an opportunity to meet some of the current students and other candidates and whilst you may find it hard to get a good night's sleep in a strange bed, you should try to make the most of the experience.

**Leave plenty of time to get to your first appointment.** Arrive at least half an hour earlier than you planned to. You do not want to turn up stressed and sweating. Transport links to both universities are excellent and generally reliable but it's always worth assuming the worst case scenario and arriving with plenty of time to spare.

**Print off a map** so you know your college's location and make sure you have enough money to get a taxi in case you arrive late or get lost.

**Have the phone number of the Admissions Office on your mobile** so you can let them know if you're delayed.

**Know where your interview is taking place**. When you arrive and are given the location of your interview room, go and find out exactly where it is. Oxbridge colleges can be confusing to navigate around and many a candidate has arrived 10 minutes late to a 20-minute interview because they couldn't locate the right staircase. Be warned.

**Dress as if you've made an effort.** You don't have to wear a suit but you should look clean and not crumpled. This is not the occasion for girls to show off their cleavage, very short skirts or shorts and probably it's best for both sexes to leave the football strip in the drawer. Brushing your hair is usually a good thing too.

**Make sure you have a book, some money for food and a charged phone.** You may spend a lot of time waiting around. This is particularly true for Oxford interviews where you may be seen by several different colleges over a number of days. The cities are expensive and you really don't want to run out of money.

**Don't relax too much!** If you meet up with friends, please don't go out and party. You will not do well at your interview the next morning and tutors will be predictably unsympathetic if you turn up the worst for wear.

## Prepare properly: The interview

There's no real mystery about what you are likely to be asked at the interview. The tutors are looking for the best qualified candidates; people whom they will enjoy teaching and who will make a contribution to their academic department. It's worth reminding yourself what qualities they are looking for in a student.

> 'The overall criteria for selection are: candidates should be able to listen effectively and present reasoned arguments orally; candidates should be able to understand and analyse written work and show they can present reasoned arguments on paper; and candidates should show motivation, interest, and creativity in the areas they have studied.'
>
> *Keble College Oxford's Admissions Department*

It's essential, therefore, that you have thought through your answers to the following questions.

- Why have you applied to study your course?
- What does your course entail, all three or four years of it?
- What did you write in your personal statement and why?

**When did you last read your personal statement?** You may not remember all the books that you said you had devoured but the tutor interviewing you will. You are VERY likely to be asked questions about your personal statement so take a copy with you and be sure you know what you wrote in it. The same applies to any written work and any supplementary answers that you submitted. Make sure you have copies with you and re-read them before the interview.

**Do you really know your subject?** Have you read the 'Introduction to . . .' on the university and college's website? Have you read around your subject beyond the obvious choices? What else have you done that proves your interest in your subject?

**Is your body language right?** Practise walking into a room, looking your parent in the eyes, smiling and say hello and shake their hand. Explain why you're doing this beforehand or they may be rather shocked. When you are called in to the interview room for real, try to greet your interviewers confidently even if you're feeling very nervous. Sit forward in your seat and look interested. You will score no extra points for slouching or seeming bored.

**Do you know the sort of questions you may be asked?** First of all, don't worry about the apocryphal mad Oxbridge questions. Most of the questions asked will be about your A level subjects and other topics that should give you an opportunity to show your mettle. There is a list of questions below that have been asked by tutors over the past few years. It's useful to look at them to give you an idea of the type of questions that might come up, but that's all. You are *much* more likely to be asked a straightforward question about your subject than any of the ones on this list.

It's also important to read a decent newspaper and keep up to date with current affairs. You may be asked your opinion on something in the news, so it's definitely worth brushing up your knowledge of current affairs in preparation.

**What happens if I can't answer their question?** Don't panic. There will often be no 'right' answer to whatever question you've been given. It's perfectly okay to ask for a few seconds to think about what you're going to say; something along the lines of 'That's an interesting question. Can I have a few moments to consider my answer?' makes you seem thoughtful, not desperate.

Really think through and rehearse the answers to the *obvious* questions to which so often even strong candidates fail to give convincing answers:

- Why do you want to read [insert subject]?
- What is it about the course that interests you? (Have you been on-line to ensure you know exactly what the course entails, all three or four years of it?)
- Why have you chosen [insert college name]? Do you know the names and special interests of the tutors who will be conducting the interview? It's all there online; make sure you find out. Knowing this makes you seem well prepared and it will make you feel more confident, because you have a little inside knowledge on the people that are interviewing you.
- Why should we give you a place to read [insert subject] rather than the nine other candidates who we are interviewing today?

Remember, no tutor will be trying to make you feel small, trick you or humiliate you. A good interviewer will allow you to demonstrate your interest in your subject and your academic potential. They are most interested in your ability to think logically and express your ideas orally.

# The big day

So the moment's finally arrived. What exactly will happen at the interview? Every experience can be different. Some colleges use a panel of interviewers, sometimes you will have consecutive interviews conducted by one individual (often the college admissions tutor, followed by one with a subject specialist) and sometimes interviewers do them in tandem.

In most cases two interviews is the standard but extra interviews may be given, or you may be sent to another college. Again, it varies.

The format will vary widely depending on subject. For some subjects (e.g. English) you may be given some prose or poetry to read before you go into your interview. You will then be asked questions on this by the tutors, who may then want to discuss the content of your personal statement – such as books you've mentioned reading or poetry you've enjoyed. For science subjects this is less common, and it is more likely that you will be given problems to solve or questions to answer. Generally these are designed to require no specific prior knowledge.

You may also be asked to attend a 'general' or 'college' interview. This is conducted by interviewers who don't teach your subject. It is possible that one of the purposes of this interview will be to see how you'll fit in with the college atmosphere and whether you are a well-rounded person who will be an asset to their college. You may be asked questions on your personal statement, about a topic of interest in the news or about your enthusiasm for your chosen subject.

Below are some examples of the sort of questions you may be asked and some students' experiences at their interviews.

### General interview questions

- Why do you want to come to this college?
- What made you want to study this subject?
- What are you intending to do in your gap year?
- Where do you see yourself in five years' time?
- Excluding your A level reading, what were the last three books you read?
- What do you regard as your strengths and weaknesses?
- What extra-curricular activities would you like to take part in at this college?

- Why did you make an 'open application'?
- Give us three reasons why we should offer you a place.
- What will you do if we don't offer you a place?
- Why did you choose your A level subjects?
- How will this degree help in your chosen career?
- How would your friends describe you?

## Subject-specific interview questions

### Anthropology/archaeology

- Name the six major world religions.
- What does Stonehenge mean to you?
- What are the problems regarding objectivity in anthropological studies?
- Why do civilisations erect monuments?
- Why should we approach all subjects from a holistic, anthropological perspective?

### Architecture

A large part of the interview is likely to be dedicated to discussing your portfolio. Be prepared to discuss the ideas, purposes and motivations behind your work. Your work should also illustrate a well-developed ability to relate two- and three-dimensional experience through drawing and 3D models. You should also be prepared to discuss your work experience. Below are some other questions that might be asked.

- Is architecture in decline?
- Could you describe a building that you recently found interesting?
- Do you have an architect whom you particularly admire? What is it about their work that you find attractive?
- If you could design a building anywhere in the world, and if money, space and time were unlimited, what would you design?

### Art history

- What do we look for when we study art? What are we trying to reveal?
- Comment on this painting on the wall.
- Compare and contrast these three images.
- What exhibitions have you been to recently?
- How do you determine the value of art?
- Who should own art?
- What is art?
- Why is art important?
- What role do art galleries and museums play in society today?
- Are humans inherently creative?

- Apart from your studies, how else might you pursue your interest in art history while at university?
- What are some key themes in the history of art?
- How has the depiction of the human form developed through the centuries?
- Who invented linear perspective – artists or architects?
- When was the discipline of art history brought to England and by whom?

## Biochemistry

- How do catalysts work?
- Describe the work of enzymes.
- Discuss the chemistry of the formation of proteins.
- Questions on oxidation, equilibria and interatomic forces.
- Questions on X-ray crystallography.
- Why do you wish to read biochemistry rather than chemistry?
- What scientific journals have you read lately? Is there a recent development in the field that particularly interests you?
- Why does most biochemistry take place away from equilibrium? (Or, How important is equilibrium to biochemical processes?)

## Biological sciences

- How does the immune system recognise invading pathogens as foreign cells?
- How does a cell stop itself from exploding due to osmosis?
- Why is carbon of such importance in living systems?
- How would you transfer a gene to a plant?
- Explain the mechanism of capillary action.
- What are the advantages of the human genome project?
- How would you locate a gene for a given characteristic in the nucleus of a cell?
- What is the major problem with heart transplants in the receiver?
- Should we be concerned about GMOs? Why or why not?
- Do cellular processes take place at equilibrium?
- How important are primary electrogenic pumps for transmembrane ion transport of organic molecules? Why are these important?
- Why do plants, fungi and bacteria utilise $H+$ gradients to energise their membranes whereas animals utilise $Na+$ gradients?

## Chemistry

- Questions on organic mechanisms.
- Questions on structure, bonding and energetics.
- Questions on acids and bases.
- Questions on isomerisation.

- Questions on practical chemical analysis.
- Describe the properties of solvents and mechanisms of salvation.

*(See also biochemistry questions.)*

## Classics

- Questions on classical civilisations and literature.
- Why do you think ancient history is important?
- How civilised was the Roman world?
- Apart from your A level texts, what have you read in the original or in translation?

## Earth sciences and geology

- Where would you place this rock sample in geological time?
- How would you determine a rock's age?
- Can you integrate this decay curve, and why would the result be useful?
- Questions on chemistry.
- When do you think oil will run out?

## Economics

- Explain how the Phillips curve arises.
- Would it be feasible to have an economy which was entirely based on the service sector?
- A man pays for his holiday at a hotel on a tropical island by cheque. He has a top credit rating and rather than cashing it, the hotelier pays a supplier using the same cheque. That supplier does the same thing with one of his suppliers and so on ad infinitum. Who pays for the man's holiday?
- What do you know about the interaction between fiscal and monetary policy?
- I notice that you study mathematics. Can you see how you might derive the profit maximisation formula from first principles?
- Tell me about competition in the television industry.
- How effective is current monetary policy?
- What are your particular interests as regards economics?
- Do you think we should worry about a balance of payments deficit?
- If you were the Chancellor of the Exchequer, how would you maximise tax revenue?
- If you had a fairy godmother who gave you unlimited sums of money, what sort of company would you start and what types of employee would you hire?
- What are the advantages and disadvantages of joining the euro?
- What are the qualities of a good economist?
- Why are you studying Economics A level?

- What would happen to employment and wage rates if the pound depreciated?
- Do you the think the Chinese exchange rate will increase?
- How does the housing market affect inflation?
- How has social mobility changed in recent times?
- How best can the government get us out of the recession?

## Engineering

- Questions on mathematics and physics, particularly calculus and mechanics.
- Questions on mathematical derivations, for example, of laws of motion.
- Look at this mechanical system sitting on my desk – how does it work?
- How do aeroplanes fly?
- What is impedance matching and how can it be achieved?
- How do bicycle spokes work?
- How would you divide a tetrahedron into two identical parts?
- What is the total resistance of the tetrahedron if there are resistors of one ohm on each edge?
- How would you design a gravity dam for holding back water?

## English

- Why might it be useful for English students to read the *Twilight* series?
- What do you consider to be the most important work of literature of the 20th century?
- Who is your favourite author?
- Apart from your A level texts, what book have you read recently, and why did you enjoy it?
- Give a review of the last play you saw at the theatre.
- Critically analyse this poem.
- How has the author used language in this text?

## Geography

- Is geography just a combination of other disciplines?
- Why should it be studied in its own right?
- If I were to visit the area where you live, what would I find interesting?
- Would anything remain of geography if we took the notion of place off the syllabus?
- How important is the history of towns when studying settlement patterns?
- Why is climate so unpredictable?
- What is the importance of space in global warming?

- Why do you think people care about human geography more than physical geography?
- What is more important, mapping or computer models?
- If you went to an isolated island to do research on the beach, how would you use the local community?
- Analyse a graph about a river. Why are there peaks and troughs?
- Look at a world map showing quality of life indicators. Explain the pattern in terms of two of the indicators.

*(See also land economy questions.)*

## History

- Discuss a historical movement that you find particularly interesting.
- How can one define revolution?
- Why did imperialism happen?
- Who was the greater democrat – Gladstone or Disraeli?
- Was the fall of the Weimar Republic inevitable?
- 'History is the study of the present with the benefit of hindsight.' Do you agree?
- Would history be worth studying if it didn't repeat itself?
- What is the difference between modern history and modern politics?
- What is the position of the individual in history?
- Would you abolish the monarchy for ideological or practical reasons?
- Why do historians differ in their views on Hitler?
- What skills should a historian have?
- In what periods has the Holy Grail been popular, with whom and why?
- Why is it important to visit historical sites relevant to the period you are studying?

## Human sciences

- Talk about bovine spongiform encephalopathy and its implications, and the role of prions in Creutzfeldt–Jakob disease.
- What causes altitude sickness and how do humans adapt physiologically to high altitudes?
- Tell me about the exploitation of indigenous populations by Westerners.
- Why is statistics a useful subject for human scientists?
- Why are humans so difficult to experiment with?
- How would you design an experiment to determine whether genetics or upbringing is more important?
- What are the scientific implications of globalisation on the world?

### Land economy

- Will the UK lose its sovereignty if it joins EMU?
- Will EMU encourage regionalism?
- Will the information technology revolution gradually result in the death of inner cities?
- What has been the effect of the Channel tunnel on surrounding land use?

### Law

- Questions on the points of law arising from scenarios – often relating to criminal law or duty of care.
- What does it mean to 'take' another's car?
- A cyclist rides the wrong way down a one-way street and a chimney falls on him. What legal proceedings should he take? What if he is riding down a private drive signed 'no trespassing'?
- X intends to poison his wife but accidentally gives the lethal draught to her identical twin. Would you consider this a murder?
- Questions on legal issues, particularly current ones.
- Should stalking be a criminal offence?
- Should judges have a legislative role?
- Do you think that anyone should be able to serve on a jury?
- Should judges be elected?
- Do judges have political bias?
- To what extent do you think the press should be able to release information concerning allegations against someone?
- Who do you think has the right to decide about euthanasia?
- How does the definition of intent distinguish murder from manslaughter?
- Can you give definitions of murder and manslaughter?
- Should foresight of consequences be considered as intending such consequences?

### Material sciences

- Questions on physics, particularly solid materials.
- Questions on mathematics, particularly forces.
- Investigations of sample materials, particularly structure and fractures.

### Maths and computation

- Questions (which may become progressively harder) on almost any area of the A level syllabus.

### Maths and further maths

- Pure maths questions on integration.
- Applied maths questions on forces.

- Statistics questions on probability.
- Computation questions on iterations, series and computer arithmetic.

## Medicine

- What did your work experience teach you about life as a doctor?
- What did you learn about asthma in your work experience on asthma research?
- How have doctors' lives changed in the past 30 years?
- Explain the logic behind the most recent NHS reforms.
- What are the mechanisms underlying diabetes?
- Why is it that cancer cells are more susceptible to destruction by radiation than normal cells?
- How would you determine whether leukaemia patients have contracted the disease because of a nearby nuclear power station?
- What does isometric exercise mean in the context of muscle function?
- What can you tell me about the mechanisms underlying sensory adaptation?
- What is an ECG?
- Why might a general practitioner not prescribe antibiotics to a toddler?
- Why are people anxious before surgery? Is it justifiable?
- How do you deal with stress?
- Why does your heart rate increase when you exercise?
- Questions on gene therapy.
- Questions on the ethics of foetal transplantation.
- Questions on biochemistry and human biology.

## Modern languages

Prepare for comprehension and translations and to answer questions on a text given immediately prior to the interview. Also be prepared to have a short conversation in the pre-studied language that you have chosen to study further at university.

- Questions which focus on the use of language in original texts.
- Describe aspects of this poem which you find interesting.
- Interpret this poem, commenting on the tone and the context of the poem.
- Why do you want to study this language and not another?
- Why is it important to study literature?
- What is the difference between literature and philosophy?
- Questions on cultural and historical context and genre in European literature.
- How important is analysis of narrative in the study of literature?
- How important is knowledge of the biography of the author in the study of their literature?
- What is language?

### Natural sciences

- What is an elastic collision?
- What happens when two particles collide – one moving and one stationary?
- What is friction?
- Questions on carboxylic acids.
- What is kinetic energy? How does it relate to heat?

### Oriental studies

- What do you know about the Chinese language and its structure?
- What are the differences between English and any Oriental language with which you are familiar?
- Does language have an effect on identity?
- Compare and contrast any ambiguities in the following sentences. 'Only suitable magazines are sold here.' 'Many species inhabit a small space.' 'He is looking for the man who crashed his car.'
- Comment on the following sentences. 'He did wrong.' 'He was wrong.' 'He was about to do wrong.'

### Philosophy

- What is philosophy?
- Would you agree that if p is true and s believes p, then s knows p?
- Was the question you have just answered about knowing or about the meaning of the word 'know'?
- Comment on these statements/questions. I could be dreaming that I am in this interview./I do not know whether I am dreaming or not./ Therefore I do not know whether I am in this interview or not. A machine has a free will. When I see red, could I be seeing what you see when you see green?
- Is it a matter of fact or logic that time travels in one direction only?
- Is our faith in scientific method itself based on scientific method? If so, does it matter?
- I can change my hairstyle and still be me. I can change my political opinions and still be me. I can have a sex change and still be me. What is it then that makes me be me?
- Can it ever be morally excusable to kill someone?

### Physics

Be prepared to answer any questions relating to the A level syllabus including the following.

- Questions on applied mathematics.
- Questions on mathematical derivations.
- How does glass transmit light?
- How does depressing a piano key make a sound?

- How does the voltage on a capacitor vary if the dielectric gas is ionised?
- How has physics influenced political thinking during the past century?

## Politics

- Can you define 'government'? Why do we need governments?
- Can you differentiate between power and authority?
- What makes power legitimate?
- What would be the result of a 'state of nature'?
- How can you distinguish between a society, a state and an economy?
- Will Old Labour ever be revived? If so, under what circumstances?
- What would you say to someone who claims that women already have equal opportunities?
- What would you do tomorrow if you were the leader of the former Soviet Union?
- How does a democracy work?
- What elements constitute the ideologies of the extreme right?
- What do you think of discrimination in favour of female parliamentarians?
- How would you improve the comprehensive system of education?
- Does the UN still have a meaningful role in world affairs?
- Is further EU enlargement sustainable?
- How important is national identity?
- Should medics pay more for their degrees?

## Psychology

- Is neuropsychology an exact science? If not, is it useful?
- Questions on the experimental elucidation of the mechanisms underlying behaviour.
- Give some examples of why an understanding of chemistry might be important in psychology.
- A new treatment is tested on a group of depressives, who are markedly better in six weeks. Does this show that the treatment was effective?
- There are records of violent crimes that exactly mimic scenes of violence on television. Does this indicate that television causes real violence?
- How would you establish the quietest sound that you can hear as opposed to the quietest sound that you think you can hear?
- Why might one be able to remember items at the beginning and end of an aurally presented list better than items in the middle?
- Could a computer ever feel emotion?
- Is it ethically justifiable to kill animals for the purpose of research?
- What is emotional intelligence?

## Sociology

- What is the value of the study of social anthropology?
- Do people need tabloids?
- How would you define terrorism?
- Do you believe in selective education? Are we participating in selective education here?
- Is it possible to pose a sociological problem without sociological bias?
- Does prison work?
- Are MPs only in it for the power?
- How has the study of race and racism changed over the past 20 years?

*(See also questions on politics and psychology.)*

## Theology

- Does moral rectitude reside in the agent, the act or its consequences?
- What, if anything, is wrong with voluntary euthanasia?
- What is the best reason that you can think of for believing in the existence of God?
- Do you think that this course could conceivably be persuasive on the issue?
- What relevance does theology have for art history?
- What relevance does archaeology have for theology?
- Can you comment on the portrayal of Jesus in John versus the other gospels?

## Veterinary medicine

- Has your work experience influenced your future career aspirations?
- Can you discuss an aspect of animal physiology which has struck you as contrasting with what you know of human physiology?
- Would our knowledge of BSE have been of value in controlling foot and mouth disease?
- Tell me about the biochemistry of DNA.
- What animal did this skull belong to?

*(See also questions on biological sciences and chemistry.)*

## Any questions?

At the end of the interview you may be asked if you have any questions to ask the interviewer(s). It is always a good idea to have a few questions up your sleeve. One or two is a good number; more than three questions is usually too many. Write them down on a notepad and bring it with you. You will appear professional and keen. You may be able to bring up one of your favourite topics that was not discussed during the main part of the interview.

If, after all your research, you still have questions about your course or college, this is the time to ask. If there was a topic covered during the interview that you didn't understand, you could enquire about where you can read more about it, or get further clarification from the interviewers themselves.

## The pooling system

The pooling system exists to ensure that all strong candidates get a good chance of being accepted to an Oxbridge college, but it means something slightly different at Cambridge and Oxford.

At Oxford, you may be 'pooled' after you have had an interview or interviews at your chosen college. This is the reason Oxford keeps applicants for several days during the interview process. You may be seen by other members of the faculty at different colleges during your stay. If you are a particularly strong candidate, academics at several colleges might ask you to interview, even if they are not at the college of your first choice and even if the academics at your preferred college already know they want to offer you a place. More often, being pooled indicates that although you are a good candidate, your chosen college does not want to offer you a place but another college may. You will then be called for interview at the college that is considering offering you a place.

At Cambridge, pooling happens after the first interview process. If you are a strong candidate, but there has been particularly high competition for places at your college, your interviewers may feel that they cannot offer you a place with them but that you deserve a place at Cambridge. They will then place you in the 'pool': a database that can be accessed by members of their faculty at different colleges. Academics at these other colleges, who may have spare places or weaker candidates, will then 'fish out' their choice of strong 'pooled' students and ask them to come for interviews at their college. These second round or 'pooling' interviews take place at the college of the academic who selects you some time in the second half of December and a few weeks after the first round of interviews. If you are pooled you still stand a chance of being accepted. Around 3,000 offers per year are made by preference colleges; 600–700 offers are made through the pool.

## Case studies: interview stories from previous applicants

### Soraya, Maths, Oxford

I arrived early, around 9.30am so that I had plenty of time to prepare for the written test. The college was full of JCR helpers, with one specifically for my subject, and they were very helpful in answering my questions. I waited around for quite a while and then took the test, which lasted two and a half hours. The test was quite hard but I think the average mark people get across the whole university was about 63%. I was glad I had practised lots of specimen papers that I downloaded online. When we finished taking the tests, we all got to know each other a bit better by playing games organised by the JCR and then in the evening we went to the pub and the cinema. This helped me to relax . . . a little! I didn't sleep too well that night but I felt okay in the morning.

Next day I had to visit the noticeboard to find out when my interviews were. I had two scheduled about four hours apart. I quite enjoyed my first interview and the tutors worked hard to make me feel relaxed. We chatted a bit about my personal statement, and then we went into the maths. I was given some problems to solve; they were a bit harder than ones I'd done in school but I kept cool and just did my best. My second interview was awful! They asked me an easy question to begin with, and then they just became more and more difficult. I just kept plodding on, trying not to show my nervousness and I kept on explaining how I was trying to solve the problems. I was miserable afterwards and I thought I'd blown it but some of the other students felt equally despondent and somehow that made me feel a bit better! I surprised myself, in the end, by finding the whole process quite good fun, and I enjoyed meeting the other applicants. Even if I hadn't been made an offer, I felt I was given a reasonable chance to prove what I could do. So be confident and just do your best.

### Adam, Economics, Cambridge

Two weeks before my interview I was sent an interview pack from Cambridge, which contained an article that I read in advance of the interview, a few maps of the college and of Cambridge, some information about the interviews and a food voucher for the food hall.

My interview was at midday. I could have stayed over the night before but I live close so I didn't. There were no designated student helpers and I got a bit lost in the college (it is very large) so I asked some people for help and directions. I would recommend going to the porter's lodge if you get very lost and they will direct you.

My first interview was the specialist interview for economics. I was interviewed by two fellows, who invited me to sit down on a couch as I entered the room where the interview took place. One interviewer sat directly in front of me and the other sat at a desk looking to the side. The interviewer who sat in front of me was the main interviewer, as the other interviewer hardly ever intervened and just took notes. The interview started with the principal interviewer asking me about what current events in the news had interested me most. I responded by talking about the euro crisis. She asked me what I thought the impact of the collapse of the euro would be on the UK. The interview continued in that same tone and style. It was a very sober, tense environment. The interview was very formal and no time was lost on discussions that did not relate to economics.

I was sent an article a couple of weeks prior to the interview and I was asked a few questions on it. The answers basically related back to my A level knowledge of the subject. Then I was given a paragraph on economics and was told to comment on it. The comment could be anything I wanted to say or thought about the paragraph. It had some errors, that were not grammatical; it rested on dubious theory such as 'if you raise taxes, people will spend more', whereas I have been taught that if you raise taxes people will spend less.

Then they asked me a mathematical problem. They gave me a whiteboard to solve it on. It was a geometric problem. The problem was that there were two pieces of carpet and you had to cover an entire room with those two pieces of carpet. The trick was you could only make one cut. This seemed to me to be impossible. I was told to do what I could and I talked through the logic of finding the solution to the problem. I was stopped after around 30 seconds. After the maths question, the interviewers asked me if I had any questions. I asked them about fiscal policy and we had a short discussion and then the interview came to an end.

My general interview was very relaxed. The admissions tutor asked me questions such as 'Why Cambridge?', 'Why this college?' and 'Tell me five words your friends would use to describe you'. I was also told to describe an object as if I was on the telephone with the admissions tutor and they could not see the object. After I described the object, he asked me why I thought he had asked that question. This laid-back style characterised the interview. It was quite an enjoyable experience. The interviewer's questions were either very general and expected or very diverse, unusual and startling.

### Melissa, Human Sciences, Oxford

I had two interviews which seemed to me more like discussions than any sort of interrogation. I had done a mock interview in order to prepare and I was pleased that I had, because its style had prepared me for the worst! When I arrived, the undergraduates at the college were incredibly helpful, as they were able to give me an insight into what my interviewers were like, and they told me what little they could remember of their own interviews, too.

The first interview lasted around 30 minutes and took place in an office just big enough for the two of us. The interviewer started by telling me about himself and some recent research he had been doing – I was so shocked by this because I had expected everything to be about me! It calmed me down, though, because it was like an ordinary conversation. He then started to ask me why I had chosen this subject over others that might have seemed more obvious for someone with my A levels. We then moved on to some technical questions. For one I had to comment on a graph showing the typical age when people die in certain countries. As I had not looked at this beforehand I had to think on my feet.

My interviewer had looked at the work I had sent in, and asked me to look at how one of the essays related to the subject I was applying for. He let me talk about this for what seemed like ages and asked me lots of things about it. He seemed interested but I couldn't really tell what he thought of me.

In the second interview, I felt far more challenged but not in a confrontational way. When I was asked a question and gave an answer the interviewer would ask me yet another question on my answer. A common question she asked was 'Why?'. It was a very exciting interview and she seemed genuinely interested in what I had to say. Although I think I tackled a lot of it well on my own, she often prompted me to get me thinking along the right lines.

Both the interviewers were very friendly and seemed to be keen to find my strengths rather than my weaknesses. On the whole, I suppose, I actually enjoyed the experience!

### Grace, History, Oxford

When I arrived at Oxford for the interview I was terribly nervous. I was taken through to a small study where two female professors were sitting. As soon as I walked in, I could sense that the atmosphere was much more relaxed than I had imagined it would be. The initial questions they asked me were drawn from points I had made in my personal statement, many of them about the Holy Grail. This immediately made me feel more relaxed, as I was confident about being able to support what I had written in my personal statement.

It was clear to me that they were not trying to trick me by asking questions about historical periods I hadn't covered. They were far more interested in the periods I had covered and were trying to engage me in debate by contradicting a number of the arguments I put forward.

After around 20 minutes, the questions became focused on an essay I had submitted prior to the interview. The questions were designed to make me look at alternative arguments to those I had used in my essay, and they made me question whether my arguments were right. However, when one of the interviewers asked me a question that seemed to have numerous correct answers, I realised that they were more interested in my ability to analyse different points of view.

I enjoyed my interview but I was not offered a place.

### Imogen, French and Italian, Oxford

I was called for an interview about 10 days before the provisional date, but the letter did nothing except confirm that I had been called. There were no times or details given. Upon arrival at Oxford, the night before the interviews began, I learnt that the next day I had a language test and an Italian interview, and a French interview the following day.

Oxford prefers not to allow candidates to make their own way to interviews, in case they get lost, so each college has a general waiting room and a group of current undergraduate helpers to accompany everyone. On the morning of the test, all the modern linguists gathered in the waiting room, and we were shown to classrooms where we had to take a grammar test in each of the languages we were applying for, except those we were intending to study from scratch. I sat tests in French and Italian, lasting an hour in total, and consisting of translation and multiple choice questions.

My Italian interview took place at Balliol (I applied to St Anne's), because there is no Italian fellow at St Anne's. A student helper took me to Balliol, and I was given an Italian poem to look at. This was discussed in my interview and I was asked to talk about subjects I had brought up in my personal statement. We then discussed various books I had read and, surprisingly, did not speak any Italian.

I had one interviewer for the first Italian interview. This was a very strange interview. I was given an Italian poem (*Canzonetta sulle sirene catodiche* by Magrelli) to read and make notes on before I was called in.

- I had to describe aspects of the poem which I found interesting.
- I was then asked to summarise my personal statement as he hadn't seen it before.
- Then he asked me why I thought that Primo Levi was a good writer, told me that his book was originally rejected by Natalia Ginzburg and asked what I felt about that.
- The conversation then moved on to Dante, and he wanted to know how I had approached my study of 'L'Inferno', and which of the canti I had enjoyed.
- I was then given the opportunity to ask him a question.

The second part of the interview consisted of a discussion of a poem and I had two interviewers. When I met the interviewers they gave me a poem to read in English.

- Again, the poem was discussed in depth, but this time I was pushed to interpret bits which were harder to understand, rather than just comment on bits I liked.
- The interviewer then picked up on the Primo Levi in my personal statement, and asked me what I thought of the quote 'After Auschwitz, no more poetry', with reference to the philosophy I studied at school.
- There was a brief conversation in Italian, focusing on current affairs and places I had visited in Italy.
- Again I was allowed to ask a question.

The next morning I had a French interview at St Anne's. Again I was given a passage to read, again in English, which was discussed with one of the interviewers.

There was a conversation in French with a second interviewer, which covered some literature and my reasons for studying French. Lastly, the third interviewer asked some slightly more in-depth questions about the importance of literature, and the relationship between literature and philosophy (I had made some references to philosophy in my personal statement).

I had three interviewers for my first French interview. I was given another passage in English; it was an extract from the works of Edgar Allen Poe.

- I was asked questions about the tone of the passage, what situation I thought the extract was taken from and how I felt the episode would conclude.
- Then we had a conversation in French – why I wanted to study French as opposed to any other language, what I felt the themes were in the film *Jules et Jim* by Francois Truffaut (the essay I sent in was based on this film) and what I felt the film said about the difference between the French and the Germans during the war.
- I was asked a series of questions, including: Why is it important to study literature? What is the difference between literature and philosophy? What French book had I recently read that I enjoyed? I talked about *La Princesse de Cleves*.

My second interview for French had two interviewers. This time I was given a poem to read in French. There was a note at the top saying that I should try to understand the poem, but not to worry if I didn't know all the vocabulary, because I would be asked which bits of the poem I found most interesting and was not expected to understand it all.

However, I was then fired a series of questions on every verse of the poem, and interrupted during every answer to be further questioned on why I thought that, where I was getting my information from, and could I give more examples to back up my point. Luckily, I had been placed in a library to read through the passage, and so had looked up all the unfamiliar vocabulary. The moral of the story – don't believe the kindly worded instructions!

One of the interviewers then said he was intrigued as to my interest in Ronsard, and we discussed where the major Petrarchian influences were in the poetry.

Then followed a French conversation where I had to talk about my work placement in Le Touquet, and what I thought the differences were between French and British holidaymakers.

I had been told that I would be allowed to leave Oxford at 10am the following morning, but that some candidates would be required to stay until later the next day to attend interviews at other colleges.

### Madeleine, Modern and Medieval Languages, Cambridge

Shortly after I had sent off my UCAS form, Cambridge contacted me by letter to give me details of the written work they required, which in my case was two essays: one for Latin and one for Italian. I wrote an essay in English for the Latin requirement, and a short essay based on an A level topic in Italian. These essays were due early in November.

I was then called to interview, again by letter, which arrived roughly halfway through November, and was told all the details and times of the tests and interviews I would be expected to sit, which all took place on one day in the first half of December.

I stayed at the college the night before my interviews, due to an early start the next day, which I would highly recommend as it gives one the opportunity to get used to the surroundings, talk to current students and it means that it isn't a great rush in the morning before the interview.

I had to sit a test first, and as a language applicant I had to choose one of my languages in which to answer. In my case, it had to be Italian, but as it turned out, very little of the test was actually in the foreign language. There was a passage to be read, in English, which I had to summarise in a foreign language (Italian), and then I had to answer a very broad essay question in English. The test lasted an hour.

My first interview was a couple of hours later, so I took the opportunity to have lunch with some friends who were also applying to other colleges, whilst making sure I left myself plenty of time to get to the interview, which was for the Latin side of my application. I was given some Latin poetry to read, try to understand and analyse, and this was then discussed in the interview. I was also questioned about the essay I had sent in, and was given some general questions about why I had applied for the course and what my gap-year plans were. In this particular interview, there were two interviewers.

Following this was my Italian interview, which was conducted by one person only. Again, I was given a passage to try to understand and talk about, and then we discussed the literature that I was studying for my A2. Finally, she asked me a couple of questions in Italian to test my standard of speaking, focusing on where I had visited in Italy.

After this, I was free to leave, with nothing else to do but wait for the result. At Cambridge the results are all given out on one day, shortly after Christmas, and this date is stated in advance. There will be one of three possible results given on this day, either an acceptance, a rejection or the news that you have been placed in the 'winter pool', which means that there is a possibility that another college will accept you, based on the strength of your UCAS application. Acceptance or rejection from this pool can be held until as late as the end of January, during which time there is the possibility of being called for further interviewing.

## The 'post-mortem'

Try not to dwell on how it went. Admission tutors often say that students who think they have done badly in fact have acquitted themselves very well . . . and vice versa. Sometimes a lengthy interview and a good grilling will mean that they've given you a fighting chance to show your true colours.

I like to tell students the story of a candidate who came out of her interview and phoned her school teacher to report back on how her interview had gone. She told him that she had been given a poem to read and analyse and when she went into her interview she announced that she wasn't sure who had written it but she knew by the style of the writing that it had to be a woman. She then spent half her interview justifying her position. The teacher was silent on the other end of the line until he finally confessed that he knew the poem very well and in fact it was written by a man. Cue many tears of frustration and embarrassment.

Three weeks later, this student was offered a place to read English at Oxford. Remember, they are not looking at how much you know now but your potential. Tutors want students who display enthusiasm for their subject, along with a natural flair and ability. They want people who aren't afraid of putting forward their point of view, as long as they can justify it. Ultimately, they want students who will be fun and challenging to teach.

# 10 | Non-standard applications

This chapter deals with 'non-standard' applications from international students and mature students.

## International students

International students are welcome at both Oxford and Cambridge and are valued members of the student population. At Cambridge, there are over 17,000 students at the University, including around 1,000 international students from over 120 different countries studying undergraduate courses.

At Oxford international students currently come from 138 countries and make up a third of the student body, including 14% of full-time undergraduate students and 63% of full-time postgraduates.

If you have read the previous chapters in this book, you will know that both universities offer a distinctive form of undergraduate education.

Students apply for a three or four-year degree in one to three subjects and they study those subjects exclusively. English universities typically do not have 'general education' or 'core curriculum' degrees that, for example, require humanities students to do science courses. The important admission criterion is excellent academic achievement. Oxford and Cambridge select on academic ability and academic potential, evinced by secondary school results (examination results and/or predicted grades), a personal statement, an academic reference and, if required, an admissions test or written work.

Teaching is by the tutorial system. Students attend lectures and seminars, and have practical laboratory sessions in the sciences but the heart of the Oxbridge teaching method is a weekly meeting with the student's tutor – typically a leading academic – and one or two other students to engage in an intensive exchange of ideas about the week's work.

All Oxford and Cambridge undergraduates live, eat and study in one of the universities' residential colleges or permanent private halls. These small communities of typically 30–70 academics and 300–500 students from across disciplines are the focus for teaching and for social and sporting life.

Both universities are research-intensive, where academics are conducting cutting-edge research in every subject. The collegiate system allows academics and students across subjects and year groups and from different cultures and countries to come together to share ideas.

Oxford and Cambridge qualifications are recognised and valued around the world. Graduates will go on to further study and/or to work in a range of professions in some of the best companies and organisations in the world.

In order to study at Oxford and Cambridge your level of English must be of a high standard. This is measured by your performance in various different examinations including:

- the IELTS (International English Language Testing System) in which you need a score of at least 7.0 in each section (speaking, listening, writing and reading)
- the English Language GCSE examination at grade B (for Oxford) or C (for Cambridge)
- the TOEFL (Test of English as a Foreign Language) exam, scoring at least 100
- for EU students a high grade in English taken as part of a leaving examination (for example the European Baccalaureate and the Abitur) may be acceptable
- an A grade in the Cambridge Certificate in Advanced English or the Cambridge Certificate of Proficiency in English.

The level of English proficiency required depends a great deal on which subject you wish to study. If you want to apply for an essay-based subject (any of the arts or social science subjects including economics, PPE, psychology, history and English literature) your written work must be fluent. On the other hand, English language is much less important for the study of mathematics.

For information about the IELTS exam and where and when it can be taken, visit: www.ielts.org

## How much does it cost?

As an international student there are three costs you'll need to consider. These are your tuition fees, college fees and living expenses.

You will have to prove that you can finance yourself for your entire course as it's not possible for you to work during the academic session to pay your way through university. Colleges ask for financial guarantees and proof is also required when applying for a visa.

You will need to be sure of your 'fee status'. Generally speaking, in order to be considered as a 'home' student for tuition fees purposes, you need to either live in an EU member state or have indefinite leave to enter or remain in the UK. In addition, you need to have lived in the European Economic Area (EEA) for the last three years, not solely for educational purposes.

The cost of studying at a UK university for an international student is much higher than for a home student. The tuition fees at Cambridge for the academic year 2011–12 start from £11,829 for most courses, although clinical medicine costs £28,632. At Oxford, fees start at £12,700 and for clinical medicine you are asked to pay £26,500. For more information go to the following websites:

Cambridge:

- international students: www.cam.ac.uk/admissions/undergraduate/international
- financial issues for international students: www.cam.ac.uk/admissions/undergraduate/international/scholarships.html
- electronic application form: www.cam.ac.uk/admissions/undergraduate/apply/forms/coaf.pdf

Oxford:

- International Students Information and Advisory Service: www.admin.ox.ac.uk/io
- official site, including entrance requirements, international qualifications, etc.: www.ox.ac.uk/admissions/undergraduate_courses/international_students/information_for_international_applicants
- fees for international students: www.admin.ox.ac.uk/studentfunding/fees
- international student application forms from: www.admissions.ox.ac.uk/forms

## College fees

All overseas-fee-status students, and those UK/EU students who are not eligible for tuition fee support (e.g. because they are taking a second degree), normally have to pay college fees in addition to university tuition fees. The college fee covers the cost to your college of providing a range of educational, domestic and pastoral services and support. The fees vary slightly between colleges but are typically in the range of £4,400 to £5,200 per year and you should allow for increases in subsequent years.

## Living expenses

Your living expenses may be higher than for a UK student, for instance if you have to stay in Oxford or Cambridge or the UK during the vacations. The minimum resources needed per year (excluding tuition and college fees) are estimated to be approximately £8,060, depending on your lifestyle.

## Applying to Oxford and Cambridge

Applications must be made at least three months early, and, with only minor exceptions (e.g. organ scholars), are mutually exclusive for first undergraduate degrees. This means that, in any one year, candidates may only apply to Oxford or Cambridge, not both.

Cambridge conducts admissions interviews in Canada, Malaysia, Singapore, Hong Kong, PR China and India for those applicants unable to travel to Cambridge. In addition to the usual UCAS application, you will have to submit a Cambridge Overseas Application Form. See the country-specific application information on the Cambridge website for more details.

Oxford applicants will have to submit a UCAS application, take a test or occasionally submit written work specific to your chosen subject. If it's not possible for you to attend interview in person, they do arrange video conference, telephone and Skype interviews – although this is by no means guaranteed.

## The interview

Every candidate offered a place at Oxbridge will be asked to interview. Normally conducted by a tutor or don, the interview will be used to check whether the course is well suited to the applicant's interests and aptitudes, and to look for evidence of self-motivation, independent thinking, academic potential and ability to learn through the tutorial system.

Scare stories about impossible questions are rife, but with some advance practice and preparation, the interview should be treated as an opportunity for students to sell themselves rather than as something to be dreaded. Questions are not designed to catch out or embarrass candidates, but to identify intellectual potential and assess how they think and respond to unfamiliar material. To help them feel ready, students should practise being in an interview situation and answering questions based around the subject they are looking to study.

## Admissions tests

Admissions tests have come to constitute a vital part of many students' applications and are used by Oxbridge and other universities to separate the increasing numbers of students applying with top grades. Tests are now used for several subjects and include the BMAT for medicine and veterinary sciences, the ELAT for English literature, and the LNAT for law. Again, the best way for students to prepare for these is practice. Details of these tests are provided in Chapter 8.

Entry requirements vary for international students, so it's always a good idea to read the international pages of each website to ensure you don't miss out. If you don't make the final cut, don't despair. Studying at Oxbridge may be a passport to the realm of the academic elite, but unsuccessful Oxbridge applicants will easily find satisfying and equally challenging alternatives in the UK.

# Mature students

A mature student at Oxford or Cambridge is classed as anyone over 21 at the start of October in their first year. Both universities welcome applications from mature students and like everyone else who wishes to join these highly selective institutions, candidates will need to demonstrate academic ability and a firm commitment to study.

Your work experience and life skills will be considered to be relevant to your application but you must have also undertaken some type of formal academic qualifications within the three years before you apply. You will need to prove to your tutors that you will be able to cope with the demands of academic study and that you have sufficient study skills to commit to an undergraduate degree course. Many different academic qualifications are acceptable. For further information on the qualifications you would need to apply, please consult the universities' websites.

The application procedure for mature students is the same as for other students and you will have to submit an application through UCAS. Also, some subjects require you to take a written test or submit written work as part of your application. Your college will be sympathetic if you are unable to supply appropriate written material but you will need to discuss this with them directly.

Oxford and Cambridge do not accept transfer students under any circumstances. However, you can apply to take a second undergraduate degree. If you're a graduate with an approved degree from another university, you can apply to take a Cambridge BA course as an affiliated student. This means you could take the degree in a year less than usual. At Cambridge, most colleges admit some affiliated students. Some colleges do not admit affiliated students for Architecture, and only Lucy Cavendish, St Edmund's and Wolfson consider affiliated applications for Medicine or Veterinary Medicine.

### How to apply

Most Cambridge colleges accept some mature students and many have large fellowships and graduate communities that make for a very welcoming and supportive environment. Some students may prefer to apply to one of the four mature-student colleges (Hughes Hall, Lucy Cavendish, St Edmund's and Wolfson). Some colleges will not accept mature students for certain subjects, so you must check their websites carefully.

At Oxford, as a mature student, you can apply to any college. One college, Harris Manchester, and three of the permanent private halls, Blackfriars, St Stephen's House and Wycliffe Hall, take only mature students.

Both universities will be looking for academic potential and motivation just as they do for younger students and they assess each application individually. Mature applicants should not be concerned that their profile will be different. Most mature students who have the right academic background will be called for interview and they will be compared fairly against applicants from very different educational backgrounds.

You will need to show evidence of your current academic or work-related performance and give assurance that if you have taken a break from education you are fully back in the routine of dealing with a heavy and challenging academic workload.

Ideally, you will present conventional academic qualifications. If this is not possible or appropriate in your case, the colleges may accept Access, Open University and other Foundation courses. You will need to provide full details of the courses you have taken and the grades achieved and/or predicted when you apply. If you cannot find a way to provide the information on your UCAS form you will need to send appropriate documents (transcripts, mark schemes, etc.) by post at the time you apply.

You will also need to present a reference which can be written by any-body who is familiar with your current academic work. If you are not currently studying, your referee may be a current or former employer but they must be able to comment on your application and potential.

Mature students from outside the UK should check carefully the infor-mation for international students. Because of recent visa changes, if you are considering bringing dependents with you to the UK it is likely that your dependents will not be eligible for a visa.

Mature students can get information and advice from the admissions offices, as well as details about events and activities run by the universi-ties for prospective mature applicants.

- www.ox.ac.uk/admissions/undergraduate_courses/why_oxford/mature_students
- www.cam.ac.uk/admissions/undergraduate/mature

# 11 | Getting the letter

Once you've had your interview you will probably have mixed emotions about how well you have done. The majority of students have no strong feeling for whether they are likely to be successful. This is perfectly normal! It's worth remembering that admissions tutors have reported to us that often candidates feel they performed badly at interview when in fact they did very well.

Don't forget, too, that your interview is just one part of your 'package'; before the tutors make a final decision they will consider your application as a whole, which means they will look at your UCAS application and any supplementary questions, school reference, written work, specialist test and your performance at the interview. One tutor told me that at Cambridge they spend about 90 minutes considering every application. They really do their utmost to pick the best candidates and make the whole process as fair as possible.

Oxford decisions are usually sent before Christmas, and conditional offers are nearly always AAA*/AAA or very occasionally AAB at A level or equivalent.

Cambridge decisions are usually received at the beginning of January, although officially they will be posted by the end of January 2013 for those interviewed in 2012. Conditional offers are nearly always A*AA at A level or equivalent. If you have applied through the Cambridge Special Access Scheme you may be made an offer that will take into account your special circumstances.

If you have applied to study Mathematics, your offers will be dependent on your grades in two STEP Papers – three-hour maths exams taken at the end of the A level exam period, which test advanced problem solving and mathematical ingenuity rather than basic knowledge and technique.

Some students who applied to Cambridge may find that they have been pooled. This will indicate that they are strong candidates for a place at Cambridge but that there is no place available for them at their chosen college. About 20% (approximately 600 out of around 3,000) of pooled applicants are subsequently awarded a place at Cambridge. Applicants are pooled for a variety of reasons, and are categorised by the pooling college as A (strongly recommended), B (probably worth an offer), P (outstanding on paper but less impressive at interview), or S (applicant in need of reassessment).

Sometimes a college wishes to see other applicants from the pool before it fills all of its places with direct applicants – this sometimes results in several applicants being pooled and subsequently being awarded places at their original college of choice. Some are subsequently invited for interview at other colleges; if this happens the college concerned will contact you to ask you to come for an interview early in January. If another college wishes to offer you a place following the pool, you should hear from them at the start or middle of January. Otherwise, your original college will write back to you by the end of January informing you that you have been unsuccessful.

If you are unsuccessful at either university, you will receive a rejection letter in the post between December and mid-January. If this is the case for you, do not despair. Remember that there is incredibly high competition to get a place at Oxbridge. Although for many subjects one in five students interviewed are accepted, for other subjects 10 students are interviewed for one place. More than 5,000 of the unsuccessful applicants per year will have been predicted three As at A level, and are clearly intelligent and successful students.

If you are rejected, despite having a set of perfect grades and impeccable references and you want to know why, ring the admissions tutor at your chosen college and ask for feedback. If your grades are good and you are really set on claiming a place at Oxbridge, think about why you did not succeed the first time and try again. Neither Cambridge nor Oxford looks badly on students who apply twice. You may have been too young the first time or too focused on school exams to dedicate enough time to the application process. Alternatively, you may not have made an appropriate subject choice and were not passionate enough about your field. If once was enough, however, focus on your other university choices and draw on your Oxbridge experiences to help you in your preparation for future interviews.

If you did not get the grades required by Oxbridge (for example you got an AAB rather than A*AA), your conditional offer will be withdrawn. You may wish to contact the admissions tutor at your college at this point, but you should be prepared for the fact that it is unlikely you will get a second chance. Oxford and Cambridge do not look kindly on retake students, unless of course there is a real and significant reason why you did not fulfil your potential in the exams (for example, illness or a bereavement in the family).

UCAS has introduced an 'Adjustment' system whereby students who get above their predicted grades can go back to universities who rejected them and try for a place again. However, it is unlikely that this system will apply to Oxford and Cambridge since they are always extremely oversubscribed. What you could do if your exam results exceed your expectations is to reapply the following year with your excellent grades.

Remember, if you are a motivated and focused student, then you will excel at whatever university you go to, and if you love your subject, then your interest will flourish wherever you are.

### Case study: Harriet, Queens' College, Cambridge

I first applied to read English at Wadham College Oxford. I sat the ELAT in November and was pleased to be called to interview. I was predicted all A/A*s and had a good personal statement and excellent references from my teachers. I had practice interviews and my school prepared me well for the whole process. When I went up to Oxford for my interviews I was very nervous and found the experience quite stressful. I wasn't asked any awful questions and I didn't end up in tears and felt in general that both my interviews went as well as they could've done. Then came the waiting. Lots of people at my school had applied to Oxbridge so there was a sense of competition about who would get in and who wouldn't. The letter arrived in the post and I was very disappointed to learn that I hadn't been offered a place. It was difficult going back to school after the Christmas holidays and hearing other people talk about how excited they were to be going to Oxford or Cambridge the following year. Still, I picked myself up, decided I would take a gap year and went on to get two As and an A* at A level.

I chose to apply to Cambridge and felt much more at ease with the whole process second time around. Even writing a personal statement seemed much easier and I felt much more mature and sure that this was what I wanted. I was called for interview at Queens' College. I sat a college test before having a general and a subject-based interview. My subject interview, although challenging, went very well. I felt that I couldn't have performed any better and the interview overran by about 10 minutes which turned out to be a good sign. I was at work when my Mum called to say a letter had arrived in the post. She congratulated me upon opening it and discovering I had been offered an unconditional place. I was overjoyed that I would be going to Cambridge next October.

It was undoubtedly worth applying again to Oxbridge and I would encourage anyone who is rejected to have another go. Not only did I feel more prepared and mature but having sat my A levels already was a huge bonus as it meant I didn't have the worry of whether I would get my grades or not. In fact, many people I know at Cambridge got rejected from Oxbridge the first time they applied. It really makes no difference in the end. Don't be disheartened by the whole process, it is much better the second time around. If you think Oxbridge is right for you, it is worth a second try.

# Appendix 1: Timetables

## The year before you apply

### March

- Request an undergraduate prospectus and the alternative prospectus from the student unions of Cambridge or Oxford.
- Book a place at an open day.
- Research other universities to which you are considering applying.

### April

- Write the first draft of your personal statement.
- Go on an open day.

### June

- Sit your A levels.

### Summer holidays

- Ask friends and family to read your personal statement and make revisions.
- Do some work experience.

## The year in which you apply

### September

- Finalise your personal statement with your teachers.
- Visit the UCAS website (www.ucas.com) and register.
- Fill in the UCAS form (UCAS applications may be submitted from 1 September).
- Register and book a place to sit the LNAT (if you want to study law at Oxford).
- Register for the BMAT exam if you are applying for medicine (at Oxford or Cambridge) or veterinary science (Cambridge only).

## October

- The deadline for UCAS receiving your application, whether for Oxford or Cambridge, is 15 October.
- Fill in the separate Cambridge Supplementary Application Questionnaire. This will be emailed to you and must be completed by 31 October.

## Late October

- Receive acknowledgement letter from your chosen college.
- HAT (for history applicants to Oxford).
- Physics and maths for Physics Aptitude Test (PAT) (for physics or physics and philosophy applicants to Oxford).
- ELAT (for applicants to English at Oxford).
- Maths Aptitude Test (for applicants for maths or computer science to Oxford).

## November

- Sit BMAT exam in the first week of November if you are applying for medicine (at Oxford or Cambridge) or veterinary science (Cambridge only).
- Deadline for sitting LNAT (for people who want to study law at Oxford) is at the beginning of November.
- Receive letter inviting you to interview from Oxford or Cambridge and explaining if and when to submit written work. Alternatively you may receive a letter rejecting you at this point.
- Submit written work with the special form – see faculty website for details. (Work should be sent directly to the college unless you have made an 'open application', in which case send it directly to the faculty. The work should be marked by your school).

## December

- If invited, attend interviews in the first three weeks of December (see precise interview dates for your subject in the prospectus).
- You may have to sit some tests at interview.
- At Cambridge you may have to sit the TSA.
- Hear the outcome of your application from Oxford, before 25 December.

## January

- Beginning of January: applicants who have been placed in the 'winter pool' are notified (Cambridge only). This may or may not entail going to Cambridge for another set of interviews.

- Middle of January: hear the outcome of your application from Cambridge.

## June

- Sit A levels.
- After A levels sit STEP paper or AEA (maths only).

## August

- Mid-August: results day.
- If you have made your grades your place will be confirmed by the university.
- If you have not made your grades, contact the admissions tutor for your college.
- You may be sent a letter of rejection at this point.

# Appendix 2: Glossary

**Admissions tutor**
The tutor especially assigned the role of selecting candidates.

**Alumni**
People who once went to the college but who have now graduated.

**Bedders**
The person who cleans your room at Cambridge.

**Clearing**
When the A level exam results come out in August, students who do not make their offers or, alternatively, students who get much better grades than predicted, can enter the competition for places at universities that have spare places.

**Collections**
Exams sat at the beginning of each term at Oxford in the colleges.

**Collegiate system**
This term describes the fact that both Oxford and Cambridge Universities are divided into about 30 separate colleges, where students live and where their social lives are based.

**Deferred entry**
This means you would like to take a gap year (i.e. defer your entry for a year). You apply this year but will accept a place in two years' time.

**Deselected**
Some candidates will not make it to the interview; they are 'deselected' before the interview and will receive a letter of rejection.

**Director of Studies (DOS)**
Director of Studies at Cambridge University. Your DOS is an academic member of staff from your subject faculty, who is also a fellow of your college. He or she is responsible for your academic development and will meet with you at the beginning and end of each term to check on your progress and will probably be your interviewer. The DOS at Cambridge is the equivalent to a tutor at Oxford.

**Don**
A teacher at a university; in particular a senior member of an Oxbridge college.

**Exhibitions**
A scholarship you can win in recognition of outstanding work at Oxford.

**Faculty**
The department building dedicated to one particular subject, for example, the Faculty of Architecture.

**Fellow**
A fellow is an academic member of a college. Each academic in every faculty is also assigned a college; this is where their office space is located. Some more senior fellows are given responsibility for the academic achievement of the students at their college and act as the DOS (at Cambridge) or tutor (at Oxford) of a number of undergraduates.

**Fresher**
First-year undergraduate student.

**Go up**
Traditionally, instead of simply saying 'go to university', for Oxford and Cambridge the term used is to 'go up' to university.

**Hall**
One of the places where you eat your meals in college. Usually you will be offered a three-course evening meal with wine. Formal Hall is a more elaborate affair and you may be required to wear your gown.

**JCR**
Abbreviation of Junior Common Room. A common room for all undergraduate students of a given college. Each college has its own JCR.

**Norrington Table**
Oxford league table that measures each college's academic achievement at the final examinations.

**Open application**
A way of applying to either Oxford or Cambridge without specifying a college.

**Oxbridge**
The collective term for Oxford and Cambridge.

## Permanent private halls

These are like mini-colleges in Oxford; two of them – St Benet's Hall (men only) and Regent's Park College (men and women) – are for students studying any subject, but the remaining five are mainly for people who are training to be in the ministry.

## Pool

The pool is where applicants who are rejected by their first-choice college are held until another college selects them for an interview. The other college may do this for a variety of reasons, such as if they do not enough good applicants and want to find better ones, or if they want to check that their weakest chosen student is better than another college's rejected student – a sort of moderation process.

## Porter's lodge

Your first port of call at an Oxford or Cambridge college. This is where post gets delivered and where, if you get lost, they will be able to direct you – a bit like reception.

## Porters

The porters are the men and women who act like wardens of the lodge.

## Read

Instead of 'studying' a subject, the verb used is to 'read' a subject.

## SAQ

The Supplementary Application Questionnaire is sent out by Cambridge once you have submitted your UCAS application. The SAQ gives Cambridge more information about you and your application and must be completed one week after you receive it. The SAQ is filled out online and costs nothing to send; if you do not have access to email you can contact the Cambridge Admissions Office for a paper version.

## Scholar

Scholarships are usually awarded at the end of the first year for outstanding work. Oxford scholars get to wear a more elaborate gown and are given a small financial bursary (usually around £200 a year). Music scholars hold their award for the whole time they are at university.

## Scouts

The people who clean your room at Oxford.

## Subfusc

The black gown, black trousers/skirt and white shirts and black tie Oxford students must wear to take exams.

**Summon**
Another way to say 'to be called' for interview.

**Supervision**
A class held on a one-to-one basis or in a small group with your tutor (at Cambridge).

**Tompkins Table**
Cambridge league table that measures each college's academic achievement at the final examinations.

**Tripos**
Term used to describe Cambridge degree courses being divided into blocks of one or two years, called Part I and Part II.

**Tutor**
At Oxford your tutor is an academic member of staff from your subject faculty, who is also a fellow of your college. He or she is responsible for your academic development and will meet with you on a regular basis to check on your progress, and will probably be your interviewer. The DOS at Cambridge is the equivalent to a tutor at Oxford.

**Tutorial**
A class held on a one-to-one basis or in a small group with your tutor (at Oxford).

***Viva voce.***
An oral exam given when you are being considered for a First Class degree and the examiners want to ask you further questions about your exam papers.

# Appendix 3: Norrington and Tompkins Tables

**Table 3:** Norrington Table – Oxford (2011)

| College | Score | Rank |
|---|---|---|
| Merton | 75.06% | 1 |
| Christ Church | 73.94% | 2 |
| New | 73.93% | 3 |
| Magdalen | 73.62% | 4 |
| Hertford | 73.52% | 5 |
| Worcester | 72.79% | 6 |
| Wadham | 72.32% | 7 |
| Jesus | 71.79% | 8 |
| Exeter | 70.89% | 9 |
| Brasenose | 70.72% | 10 |
| St John's | 70.64% | 11 |
| Mansfield | 70.00% | 12 |
| Pembroke | 69.80% | 13 |
| University | 69.71% | 14 |
| Lincoln | 69.55% | 15 |
| Corpus Christi | 69.44% | 16 |
| Trinity | 68.28% | 17 |
| St Anne's | 68.00% | 18 |
| St Hilda's | 68.00% | 18 |
| Keble | 67.93% | 20 |
| Balliol | 67.62% | 21 |
| Lady Margaret Hall | 67.06% | 22 |
| St Hugh's | 66.92% | 23 |
| Queen's | 66.81% | 24 |
| St Catherine's | 66.41% | 25 |
| Somerville | 66.25% | 26 |
| St Edmund Hall | 66.00% | 27 |
| St Peter's | 65.86% | 28 |
| Oriel | 65.58% | 29 |
| Harris Manchester | 60.00% | 30 |

**Table 4:** Tompkins Table – Cambridge (2011)

| Position | College | Point score | % Firsts |
|---|---|---|---|
| 1 (2) | Trinity | 70.94% | 37.2% |
| 2 (1) | Emmanuel | 69.79% | 31.8% |
| 3 (4) | Trinity Hall | 68.40% | 29.3% |
| 4 (8) | Clare | 67.51% | 26.9% |
| 5 (10) | Pembroke | 67.49% | 28.9% |
| 6 (12) | Christ's | 67.41% | 27.7% |
| 7 (6) | Selwyn | 67.11% | 26.3% |
| 8 (16) | Jesus | 66.51% | 27.2% |
| 9 (5) | Magdalene | 66.22% | 23.6% |
| 10 (3) | Churchill | 66.16% | 25.1% |
| 11 (9) | St Catharine's | 65.94% | 26.7% |
| 12 (13) | Corpus Christi | 65.88% | 24.5% |
| 13 (11) | Gonville& Caius | 65.36% | 23.5% |
| 14 (17) | Queens' | 65.14% | 23.7% |
| 15 (20) | St John's | 64.30% | 22.1% |
| 16 (18) | Sidney Sussex | 64.21% | 21.0% |
| 17 (15) | Downing' | 64.02% | 19.4% |
| 18 (7) | Peterhouse | 63.51% | 22.1% |
| 19 (19) | Robinson | 63.18% | 18.6% |
| 20 (14) | King's | 63.08% | 20.9% |
| 21 (22) | Fitzwilliam | 62.62% | 20.4% |
| 22 (23) | Murray Edwards | 61.51% | 15.5% |
| 23 (21) | Girton | 61.38% | 16.3% |
| 24 (25) | Newnham | 60.96% | 13.8% |
| 25 (24) | Wolfson | 60.69% | 17.1% |
| 26 (26) | Homerton | 59.39% | 14.3% |
| 27 (27) | Hughes Hall | 59.27% | 12.7% |
| 28 (28) | St Edmund's | 56.32% | 10.8% |
| 29 (29) | Lucy Cavendish | 55.38% | 9.5% |

Figure in brackets shows previous year's position

Reprinted with kind permission of *The Independent*

# Appendix 4: Maps

## Oxford map

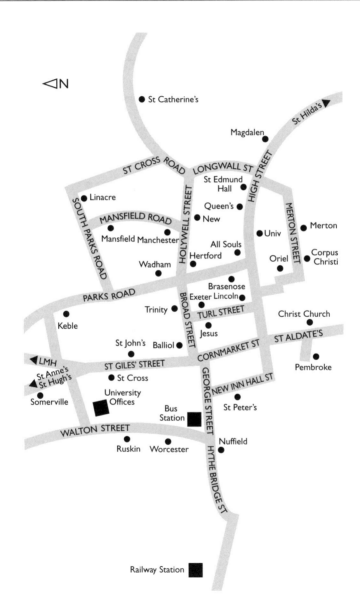

# Cambridge map

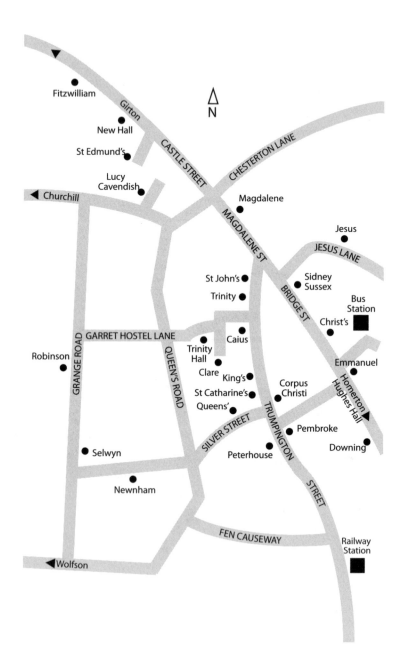